Psychological Perspectives on Religious Education

Religion and Education

Editor-in-Chief

Stephen G. Parker (*University of Worcester*)

Associate Editors

Jenny Berglund (*Stockholm University*)
Leslie J. Francis (*University of Warwick*)
David Lewin (*University of Strathclyde*)
Deirdre Raftery (*University College Dublin*)

Volumes published in this Brill Research Perspectives title are listed at *brill.com/rpre*

Psychological Perspectives on Religious Education

An Individual Differences Approach

By

Leslie J. Francis

BRILL

LEIDEN | BOSTON

This paperback book edition is simultaneously published as issue 1.2 (2019) of *Religion and Education*, DOI:10.1163/25895303-12340002.

Library of Congress Control Number: 2019920918

Typeface for the Latin, Greek, and Cyrillic scripts: "Brill". See and download: brill.com/brill-typeface.

ISBN 978-90-04-42716-7 (paperback)
ISBN 978-90-04-42717-4 (e-book)

Copyright 2020 by Leslie J. Francis. Published by Koninklijke Brill NV, Leiden, The Netherlands. Koninklijke Brill NV incorporates the imprints Brill, Brill Hes & De Graaf, Brill Nijhoff, Brill Rodopi, Brill Sense, Hotei Publishing, mentis Verlag, Verlag Ferdinand Schöningh and Wilhelm Fink Verlag. Koninklijke Brill NV reserves the right to protect the publication against unauthorized use and to authorize dissemination by means of offprints, legitimate photocopies, microform editions, reprints, translations, and secondary information sources, such as abstracting and indexing services including databases. Requests for commercial re-use, use of parts of the publication, and/or translations must be addressed to Koninklijke Brill NV.

This book is printed on acid-free paper and produced in a sustainable manner.

Contents

Psychological Perspectives on Religious Education
An Individual Differences Approach   1
      Leslie J. Francis
  Abstract   1
  Keywords   1
  Preface   1
  Introduction   2
1 Starting with Developmental Psychology   4
2 Individual Differences and Religious Affect   9
3 Personality and Religion   15
4 Sex Differences in Religion   20
5 Correlates of Religious Affect   24
6 Church Schools, Households, and Religious Formation   29
7 Attitude toward Religious Diversity   34
8 Psychological Type Theory for Ministry and Discipleship   42
9 Biblical Hermeneutics and Homiletics   47
10 Religious Orientation Theory and Motivational Styles   51
  Conclusion   57
  References   58

Psychological Perspectives on Religious Education
An Individual Differences Approach

Leslie J. Francis
University of Warwick, Coventry, UK, *leslie.francis@warwick.ac.uk*

Abstract

In this publication the contributions made by the individual differences tradition of psychology over the past 50 years to research in religious education are reviewed and assessed. In this context religious education is conceived broadly to embrace what takes place in schools, within religious communities, and within households across the age span. The opening section roots the analysis within the tradition of developmental psychology and the research that flourished in the area of religious development during the 1960s. It is from these foundations that current interest in the individual differences approach emerges. Subsequent sections examine the centrality of the attitudinal dimension of religion, discuss the place of personality in the individual differences tradition, explore sex as a core individual difference in religion, map the correlates, antecedents and consequences of individual differences in religious affect or attitudes, review research into the distinctiveness and effectiveness of church schools and the family in religious nurture, identify the factors that account for individual differences in attitude toward religious diversity, explore the relevance of the individual differences tradition for adult religious education, and explore the implications of the individual differences tradition for biblical hermeneutics and discipleship learning.

Keywords

religious education – psychology of religion – clergy studies – congregation studies – empirical theology – practical theology – pastoral theology – psychological type – individual differences – church schools

Preface

Much of my academic career has been dedicated to exploring the contribution of psychological theory and psychological research to the field of religious

© LESLIE J. FRANCIS, 2020 | DOI:10.1163/9789004427174_002

education, as this relates to children, adolescents, and adults within the context of schools, faith communities, and households. In particular I have based my research within the individual differences approach, as informed by psychology and theology. I am grateful to Stephen Parker for suggesting that I might summarise this body of research within the present publication. I also want to express my appreciation to my colleagues Emma Eccles for helping me to shape the manuscript and Judith Muskett for careful proofreading and for offering insightful editorial advice.

Research of this nature is never a solitary activity. The list of references gives credit to the number and range of colleagues who have collaborated with me across national boundaries and across religious traditions. I am indebted to them all. I am also indebted to the multiple sources of funding that have made such empirical research possible, and to the thousands of individuals (children, adolescents, and adults) who have contributed to this research by their willing participation in the studies to which I refer in this publication.

Introduction

According to Lewis Carroll, the Humpty Dumpty who thrives in wonderland and who is revealed through the looking glass is the master of language. 'When *I* use a word', Humpty Dumpty said in a rather scornful tone, 'it means just what I choose it to mean—neither more nor less'. Within the academic community, the power of punctuation is little less than the power of words. Within the wonderland of punctuation the colon reigns as sovereign. The colon may often negotiate between ambition and realism. Before the colon of this publication, the title expresses an unrealistically ambitious field, namely 'Psychological Perspectives on Religious Education'. The problem is that psychology is a vast field embracing a wide range of disciplinary approaches. Religious education is vast also, embracing both the notions of education about religions and education into religious, embracing the age span from cradle to grave, and embracing the agencies of home, school, and faith community. After the colon, the title locates the branch of psychology that will focus this publication, namely 'an individual differences approach'.

In the introduction to his book, *Personality and individual differences*, Chamorro-Premuzic (2007) sums up the distinctive contribution of the individual differences tradition within psychology in the following way.

> The study of individual differences is part of a well-established tradition in psychology that dates back more than a century. It encompasses several non-observable or 'latent' constructs, such as intelligence and

personality, which represent major sources of variation in behaviour. This makes individual differences a unique area in psychology. Whereas most psychological theories pretty much assume that everybody is the same and hence attempts to identify the universal aspects of human behaviour, individual difference theories are concerned with *differences* between people, or what makes everyone unique.

CHAMORRO-PREMUZIC, 2007, p. 1

When I began my doctoral programme in the field of psychological research and religious education in 1972, the field was dominated by developmental psychology, by the influence of Piaget (see, for example, Flavell, 1963), and by the pioneering work of Goldman in his two influential books, *Religious thinking from childhood to adolescence* (1964), and *Readiness for religion* (1965). In that generation it was almost inevitable that I grounded my doctoral work in the developmental tradition working to the title, *An enquiry into the concept 'Readiness for religion'* (Francis, 1976). It was during the process of sifting through the results of the 200 interviews that I had conducted with my modified form of the Goldman interview schedule that I lost faith in the tradition and sought inspiration elsewhere. The individual differences approach seemed to have potential and over 40 years later I am still mining that potential.

I start this publication in Section 1 by re-visiting the developmental tradition with which I started and by giving due credit to the foundation laid by Goldman and on which I subsequently built. Section 2 examines different dimensions of religion discussed by the individual differences approach and introduces the centrality of the attitudinal dimension of religion. Section 3 discusses the place of personality in the individual differences tradition and draws attention to the importance of Eysenck's three-dimensional model of personality for research in religion. Section 4 discusses sex as a core individual difference in religion. Section 5 maps the correlates, antecedents, and consequences of individual differences in religious affect or attitudes. Section 6 reviews research into the distinctiveness and effectiveness of church schools and into the primacy of the family as the core agency in religious nurture. Section 7 turns attention to identifying the factors that account for individual differences in attitude toward religious diversity. Section 8 explores the relevance of research in the individual differences tradition for adult religious education, including shaping religious leaders and ministry. Sections 9 and 10 continue the theme of adult religious education by exploring the implications of the individual differences tradition for biblical hermeneutics and homiletics (Section 9) and by exploring the implications of religious orientation theory and motivational styles for understanding differences in church congregations and preferences for preaching styles (Section 10). The publication concludes in the usual way with a thorough list of references that may prove useful to future researchers working in the field.

1 Starting with Developmental Psychology

When I began my doctoral programme in the field of psychological research and religious education in 1972, the field was dominated by developmental psychology and by the work of Goldman (1964, 1965). The theoretical framework for Goldman's (1964) book, *Religious thinking from childhood to adolescence*, was grounded in the work of Piaget (see, for example, Flavell, 1963) as reflected in studies like Piaget (1969, 1970, 1972, 1973). In essence Piaget's research was concerned with the development of cognitive processes, with the way in which the ability to think undergoes qualitative changes during childhood and adolescence. The theory distinguishes among three developmental stages in thinking which are characterised as pre-operational thinking, concrete operational thinking, and formal operational thinking. What Goldman set out to do was to apply a theory which had already proved useful in other curriculum areas to the field of religious education.

In order to test Piagetian theory within the field of religious education Goldman employed the method of clinical interview. This technique meant that Goldman interviewed children and young people one at a time, following a structured sequence of questions. The interviews allowed Goldman to probe the answers given and to test their understanding and grasp of what they said. Goldman conducted 200 interviews with ten boys and ten girls within each age group from the age of six to 17 (with 15-, 16-, and 17-year-olds considered as one age group).

The conversation in the interviews was driven by two main devices. First, the children and young people were asked to listen to three tape-recorded bible stories: Moses and the burning bush, the Israelites crossing the Red Sea, and the Temptations of Jesus in the wilderness. After each story they were asked probing questions about their understanding of the narratives. For a full appreciation of this part of the research, it is necessary to look at one of the three bible passages used and to examine the questions employed to probe the passage. Here is the way in which Goldman presented the story of the burning bush, not by using a recognised translation of the account in the bible, but by creating his own paraphrase.

> A man called Moses was one day looking after a flock of sheep in a rather lonely place, close to a mountain.

Suddenly an angel appeared to Moses in a flame of fire, out of the middle of a bush. The curious thing was that the fire was burning away, but the bush itself wasn't burnt.

Moses said to himself: 'I must go and look at it closer, to see why the bush isn't burned.' Now when God saw Moses come nearer to the bush, God called out from the middle of the bush, 'Moses! Moses!' And Moses, not knowing who it was calling, said, 'Here I am.'

And God said: 'Come no closer and take off your shoes. You are standing on holy ground.' Then God spoke again and said, 'I am your father's God, and the God of great men like Abraham and Isaac and Jacob.'

Then Moses hid his face, for he was afraid to look at God.

> GOLDMAN, 1964, pp. 253–255

Here are five of the eight questions which Goldman asked about this passage to probe the children's 'religious thinking' about the story. Only answers to the three questions marked with an asterisk were interpreted to assess Piagetian stages of thinking.

It says at the end of the story that Moses hid his face because he was afraid to look at God.
  – Why do you think Moses was afraid to look at God? Any other reason(s)?*
  – Should he have been afraid to look at God? Yes/No/d.k. Why?/Why not?
  – Would you have been afraid? Yes/No/d.k. Why?/Why not?
Supposing Moses had got over his fear and looked at God.
  – What do you think he would have seen?
  – What sort of man, face, expression, light, fire, angel?
Why do you think the ground upon which Moses stood was holy?*
  – Is God everywhere? Yes/No/d.k./unsure. Then is everywhere holy, or just special places?
  – Is this ground holy? Yes/No/d.k./unsure. Why?/Why not?
How would you explain the bush burning, and yet not being burned?*
  – How do you think such a thing could happen?*
If Moses had been deaf, do you think he would have heard God calling him?
  – Why/Why not?
  – If there had been other people near, would they have heard God calling Moses?
  – Why/Why not?

Second, the children and young people were asked to look at three pictures, one at a time, and to answer questions about the pictures. The pictures were used as a 'projective device'. Each picture presented a child of the same sex and age as the child being interviewed. The child being interviewed was then asked questions about the child in the picture. The assumption is that when answering for the child in the picture, the interviewee is answering about himself or herself. The three pictures showed a family going to church, a boy or a girl at prayer, and a boy or a girl looking at a mutilated bible.

Using the statistical technique of scalogram analysis, Goldman interpreted the findings of these interviews as evidence for the view that religious thinking develops through an invariant sequence of stages during childhood and adolescence in line with the Piagetian model. This analysis was based on the students' answers to just five of the many questions asked in the interviews (three from Moses and the burning bush, one from the Israelites crossing the Red Sea, and one from the Temptations of Jesus). On the basis of this analysis, Goldman concluded that before the onset of formal operational thinking, occurring from the age of 13 or 14 upwards, religious thinking was seriously restricted.

To understand Goldman's conclusion it is important to be clear about his definition of 'religious thinking'. For Goldman, religious thinking means the capability to think logically about religion. The problem Goldman faced in applying this definition was to distinguish between the *processes* of religious thinking (with which Piagetian psychology is mainly concerned) and the *content* of religious thinking (with which theology is mainly concerned). Re-reading Goldman's study, it seems that he valued a liberal theological position more highly than a conservative theological position.

The year after publishing *Religious thinking from childhood to adolescence* (1964), Goldman published a second book *Readiness for religion* (1965), which proposed a fresh approach to religious education, based not on scripture but on life themes. This approach was consistent with the findings from his research, but could not be derived logically from the research. *Readiness for Religion* was influential in changing the face of religious education in county schools, beginning with the new West Riding Agreed Syllabus (West Riding, 1966).

Goldman's research method stimulated a number of other researchers to build on his pioneering work, applying the same theoretical framework to specific aspects of religious development, including Bull (1969), Brisco (1969), Kingam (1969), Miles (1971), Greer (1972), Richmond (1972), Whitehouse (1972), Fagerlind (1974), and Morely (1975). For example, Bull (1969) followed the path from religion to morality in his study of *Moral judgement from childhood to adolescence*. Whitehouse (1972) selected the biblical narrative of Zacchaeus, to avoid the emphasis on miraculous events which was present in the three stories used by Goldman, and interviewed 20 first-year and 20 fourth-year junior students from two closely matched county and Roman Catholic schools. Related studies used the clinical interview technique to explore ideas of eucharistic presence (Jaspard, 1971), the priest's occupations (Dumoulin, 1971), themes of resurrection and hell (Darcy & Beniskos, 1971), and the concept of God (Nye & Carlson, 1984).

Goldman's research was not only the most influential study of the 1960s, it was also the most controversial. The debate about Goldman's research included studies by Howkins (1966), Hyde (1968, 1984), Cox (1968), Godin (1968), Langdon (1969), Attfield (1974), Murphy (1977), Roy (1979), Greer (1980), McGrady (1982), Maas (1985), Gobbel and Gobbel (1986), Petrovich (1988), and Slee (1986a, 1986b, 1990). These studies have criticised Goldman for over-reliance on the Piagetian framework or for misuse of this framework; for distorting the biblical material used to stimulate the interviews or for failing to select a proper range of biblical material; for confusing analysis of stages of thinking with styles of theological preference or for giving unfair preference to a liberal theological perspective; for misunderstanding or misapplying statistical techniques to qualitative data; and for failing to demonstrate a sound link between his research findings and curriculum recommendations.

For example, Slee (1986b) examined the two methods of data analysis which formed the basis of Goldman's developmental theory of religious thinking: content analysis and scalogram analysis. She concluded that both methods were subject to grave limitations and weaknesses and cannot substantiate Goldman's theory of religious thinking development. Francis (1979a) suggested that more careful consideration be given to the meaning of the phrase 'the development of religious thinking'. He argued that this phrase disguised three very different notions, which he distinguished as *thinking about religion*, *thinking religiously*, and *thinking in religious language*. Each of these different constructs requires a different research method. Goldman's research, Francis argued, was concerned solely with thinking about religion and should not be generalised as if it also embraced the other two notions.

At the same time other empirical studies, working within a range of research traditions, have suggested that primary school children are capable of a much richer and more developed understanding of religious ideas and concepts than those with which Goldman credited them, including Van Bunnen (1965), Gates (1976), and Murphy (1979).

Goldman's research raised a number of questions about the correlates of the development of religious thinking, concerning issues like the comparative influence of home background and school curriculum on promoting or inhibiting the development from one stage to the next. The problem with Goldman's method of clinical interview is that, since each interview takes so long, it becomes very costly to build up a database of sufficient size to enable the statistical modelling of potential influences. Peatling (1973, 1974, 1977) proposed an imaginative solution to this problem by developing a criterion referenced multiple-choice pencil and paper test, known as *Thinking about the Bible* (*TAB*). This instrument was designed to generate scores on six scales of religious thinking. Peatling employed the same version of the same three bible stories as Goldman: Moses and the burning bush, Crossing the Red Sea, and the Temptations of Jesus. After listening to a tape recording of each story, the children and young people were presented with a series of four multiple-choice questions. Each question was followed by four possible answers. The children and young people were asked to choose the answer they liked most (to be marked M) and the answer they liked least (to be marked L).

The four possible answers to each question were selected as being representative of four levels of religious thinking, styled as *very concrete*, *concrete*, *abstract*, and *very abstract*. Each time, these four levels of thinking were arranged in random order. When scoring the instrument, six scores were produced for each student. In addition to the very concrete, concrete, abstract, and very abstract scores, the very concrete and concrete scores were combined to produce a *total concrete* score, while the very abstract and abstract scores were combined to produce a *total abstract* score.

Peatling's original study, based on 1,994 students in the USA, suggested that abstract religious thinking was not attained until later than Goldman's estimate of 14 years two months. Peatling's *Thinking about the Bible* measure has been reapplied in the USA by Peatling and Laabs (1975), Peatling, Laabs, and Newton (1975), and Hoge and Petrillo (1978), in Finland by Tamminen (1976, 1991), in Northern Ireland by Greer (1981), in the Republic of Ireland by McGrady (1990, 1994a, 1994b), and in England, Northern Ireland, and the Republic of Ireland by Kay (1981e).

Peatling's measure, *Thinking about the Bible* has been significantly criticised from both conceptual and psychometric perspectives. For example, Greer (1983) argued that item selection within the forced-choice format might be influenced not only by preferences for stages of thinking but also by variability in readability and in theological perspective. He also maintained that, while the test appears to give a useful measure of the level of religious thinking in which *groups* are operating, it does not seem to be a valid indicator of the level of religious thinking revealed by the interview of *individual* students. McGrady (1983) argued that the six scales proposed by the instrument to measure underlying

PSYCHOLOGICAL PERSPECTIVES ON RELIGIOUS EDUCATION 9

developmental constructs both misrepresent Goldman's categories, and quantify the results of the measurement in a manner inconsistent with Piagentian stage theory.

In spite of such criticisms, Peatling's work represents a significant milestone in the movement of psychological research in religious education into the measurement paradigm so distinctive of the individual differences tradition.

2 Individual Differences and Religious Affect

The individual differences approach within the psychology of religion begins by distinguishing among and attempting to operationalise different dimensions of religion. One powerful model for distinguishing between different dimensions of religion well-established in the social sciences discusses the dimensions of affiliation, belief, practice, and attitudes. Each of these dimensions is of theological significance and of social significance, and may be treated somewhat differently by empirical theologians and by social scientists of religion.

Religious affiliation is a measure of belonging and of self-identification with a religious tradition. This is the level of information that it is acceptable to assemble as part of a public census. For social scientists, religious affiliation is conceptualised as an aspect of individual identity, alongside, say, factors like sex and ethnicity. Religious affiliation does not function as a secure predictor of other dimensions like religious belief and religious practice, but nonetheless it remains of key interest to empirical theologians and to social scientists. For empirical theologians it is important to consider the theological significance of claiming affiliation without adopting the practice or belief systems of a religious tradition. For social scientists it is important to recognise the empirical evidence for the enduring power of religious affiliation (in the absence of practice and belief) to predict individual differences of considerable social significance. While social scientists may find it acceptable to group broad faith traditions (as demonstrated by inclusion of the broad category 'Christian' within the 2001 and 2011 census in England and Wales), empirical theologians may be much more aware of the implications of theological differences within the Christian tradition.

Religious belief is a measure of the cognitive component of religion. The ways in which religious belief is conceptualised and measured may vary considerably between theological and social scientific traditions. Individual differences in religious belief may be expressed very differently by the theologically naïve and those who are theologically trained and sophisticated. Early attempts by social scientists to conceptualise and to measure Christian belief tended to imagine that conservative belief defined the recognised norm. Such conceptualisation worked well to characterise those who scored high, on such instruments, as conservative Christian believers. It remained more problematic, however, to characterise low scorers on such instruments, where potential confusion exists between atheists, agnostics, and liberal believers. A further confusion arises when the content of belief is confused with the manner in which belief is held. Conservative belief does not equate with dogmatic belief. Empirical theologians may be much more aware of the theological complexity involved in defining and calibrating the dimensions of Christian belief.

Religious practice is a measure of the behavioural component of religion. Again, the ways in which religious practice is conceptualised and measured may vary considerably between theological and social scientific traditions. Distinctions, too, need to be made between the observance of public practice (say, church attendance) and the observance of private practice (say, personal prayer). Early attempts by social scientists to assess the psychological correlates of prayer concentrated primarily on assessing the frequency of prayer without differentiation among the different types or forms of prayers. Empirical theologians may be much more aware of the complexity and theological differences of prayer within religious traditions.

Attitude toward religion is a measure of the affective component of religion. A very long tradition in social psychology has developed considerable conceptual and methodological sophistication in defining and operationalising the attitudinal dimension of religion. This domain is concerned with how individuals feel (negatively and positively) toward religion. Early attempts by social scientists to provide measures of attitude toward religion may have been distracted by over-emphasis on the outward and more visible aspects of religious traditions. Empirical theologians may be more aware of the inward and more spiritually salient aspects of religious traditions.

Reflecting on these four dimensions of religion in the early 1970s, Francis (1976) recognised that the attitudinal dimension was able to get closer to the heart of religion within individual lives and also that the measurement of attitude carried a number of important advantages over the measurement of affiliation, belief, or practice.

First, although affiliation has been shown to be of conceptual and empirical value within social sciences, there are significant limitations for this construct within the individual differences approach. On the one hand, the level of measurement achieved is only that of discrete categories. Individuals are located either within one category or another. On the other hand, affiliation categories take on significantly different meanings within different denominational groups. While nominalism is high, say, among Anglicans; in another group, say among Baptists, nominalism is low.

Second, although practice may be easy to conceptualise and to measure on ordinal or (possibly) interval scales, the actual meaning of practice may vary according to a range of constraints. For example, an irreligious young person may attend church because of family pressures, while a highly religious elderly person may stay away from church because of health-related problems. Moreover, practice may convey different significances within different denominational environments.

Third, although belief may be open to clear conceptualisation and (in some senses) refined measurement on (probably) interval scales, the formulation of indices of religious belief are conceptually complex (both theologically and psychologically). It is this formulation of measures of belief which may distinguish one denominational group from another, the theologically educated from the theologically naïve, and so on. While such issues are of central importance to certain fields of theological enquiry, they may simply provide distraction to the broader individual differences approach concerned with comparative research dealing with the personal and social correlates of religion.

As a deep-seated underlying construct concerned with affective response to religion (favourably toward or negatively against), a well-developed attitude scale is able to calibrate individual differences in religiosity across age groups and across denominational divides. After reviewing existing research in the field of measuring attitude toward religion during childhood and adolescence (Garrity, 1960; Jones, 1962; Johnson, 1966; Alatopoulos, 1968; Esawi, 1968; Taylor, 1970; Turner, 1970; Povall, 1971; Lewis, 1974; Westbury, 1975; Russell, 1978), Francis (1978a) recognised that the problem in integrating and synthesising the findings from these studies resulted from the diversity of measuring instruments used. As a consequence, in a paper entitled 'Measurement Reapplied', Francis (1978b) invited other researchers to collaborate with him in using the same measuring instrument, the Francis Scale of Attitude toward Christianity, in building up a secure basis of empirical information regarding the correlates, consequences, and antecedents of a positive attitude toward Christianity. By agreeing on the use of the same measure, colleagues could be clear that their independent studies fitted together to build an integrated tapestry of research concerning the contributions being made to individual lives of the form of religiosity being accessed by the Francis Scale of Attitude toward Christianity.

This 24-item scale was developed after systematically testing the five different approaches to attitude scaling proposed by Thurstone (1928), Likert (1932), Guttman (1944), Edwards (1957), and Osgood, Suci, and Tannenbaum (1957) among different age groups. The Likert method of scaling emerged as the most reliable and robust over the school-age population. The items are concerned with the students' affective responses to God, Jesus, bible, prayer, and church, assessed on a five-point scale, ranging from agree strongly, through not certain, to disagree strongly. The scientific basis for confidence in the assertion that studies conducted in different contexts could be joined together rested on the demonstration that the instrument functioned with comparable degrees of reliability and validity among different age groups, among different denominational groups, and in different countries.

This programme of establishing the reliability and validity of the Francis Scale of Attitude toward Christianity began in English-speaking contexts. The reliability and validity of the scale have been supported by studies among school students in England (Francis, 1987a, 1988, 1989a; Adamson, Shevlin, Lloyd, & Lewis, 2000; Lewis, Cruise, McGuckin, & Francis, 2006; Lewis, Cruise, & Lattimer, 2007; Francis, Lankshear, & Eccles, 2017), Kenya (Fulljames & Francis, 1987a), Nigeria (Francis & McCarron, 1989), Northern Ireland (Francis & Greer, 1990a; Greer & Francis, 1991), and Scotland (Gibson, 1989a; Gibson & Francis, 1989). Another series of studies has supported the reliability and validity of the scale among adults in Australia (Hancock, Tiliopoulos, & Francis, 2010), Australia and Canada (Francis, Lewis, Philipchalk, Brown, & Lester, 1995), England (Francis & Stubbs, 1987; Francis, 1992a), the Republic of Ireland (Maltby, 1994), Northern Ireland (Lewis & Maltby, 1997; Lewis, Cruise, & McGuckin, 2005), South Africa (Francis, Kerr, & Lewis, 2005), the USA (Lewis & Maltby, 1995a), and Wales (Robbins, Francis, & Williams, 2003). In addition to the full 24-item form of the Francis Scale of Attitude toward Christianity, a seven-item short form has been developed and tested among primary school pupils (Francis, 1992b), secondary school pupils (Francis, Greer, & Gibson, 1991), and adults (Francis, 1993a; Francis, Lewis, Philipchalk, Lester, & Brown, 1995; Maltby & Lewis, 1997; Lewis, Shevlin, Lloyd, & Adamson, 1998). There is also a five-item version proposed and tested by Campo-Arias, Oviedo, and Cogollo (2009), Miranda-Tapia, Cogollo, Herazo, and Campo-Arias (2010), Cogollo, Gómez-Bustamante, Herazo, and Campo-Arias (2012), Ceballos, Suescun, Oviedo, Herazo, and Campo-Arias (2015), and Campo-Arias, Herazo, and Oviedo (2017), and a four-item version proposed and tested by Campo-Arias and Ceballos-Ospino (in press).

In order to facilitate further cross-cultural studies within the psychology of religion, the Francis Scale of Attitude toward Christianity has also been translated into a number of different languages, including: Arabic (Munayer, 2000), Chinese (Francis, Lewis, & Ng, 2002; Tiliopoulos, Francis, & Jiang, 2013), Czech (Francis, Quesnell, & Lewis, 2010), Dutch (Francis & Hermans, 2000),

Estonian (Elken, Francis, & Robbins, 2010), French (Lewis & Francis, 2003, 2004), German (Francis & Kwiran, 1999a; Francis, Ziebertz, & Lewis, 2002), Greek (Youtika, Joseph, & Diduca, 1999; Nazar, 2019), Italian (Crea, Baiocco, Ioverno, Buzzi, & Francis, 2014), Norwegian (Francis & Enger, 2002), Portugese (Ferreira & Neto, 2002), Romanian (Francis, Ispas, Robbins, Ilie, & Iliescu, 2009), Serbian (Flere, Francis, & Robbins, 2011), Slovakian (Lewis, Adamovová, & Francis, 2008), Slovenian (Flere, Klanjsek, Francis, & Robbins, 2008), Spanish (Campo-Arias, Oviedo, Dtaz, & Cogollo, 2006), Swedish (Eek, 2001), and Welsh (Evans & Francis, 1996; Francis & Thomas, 2003).

As a consequence of these studies, the horizons for comparative research in religious education has been enlarged against the background of a common religious heritage and an instrument that has the capability of operationalising the construct of attitude toward Christianity in a variety of languages.

The third generation of studies conducted within this tradition began to explore how the basic attitudinal construct accessed by the Francis Scale of Attitude toward Christianity could be translated within other religious traditions. In this way it becomes possible to test whether the correlates, antecedents, and consequences of individual differences in attitude toward Christianity remain consistent within other religious traditions. Thus, having established the usefulness of the attitudinal dimension within the individual differences approach to investigating the personal and social correlates of religiosity within a Christian or post-Christian context, an international group of scholars has begun to examine the potential for developing parallel instruments shaped within other religious contexts, namely (in chronological order of development), Islam, Judaism, Hinduism, and Sikhism.

The core characteristics of the Francis Scale of Attitude toward Christianity are that it focuses on the affective response to the Christian tradition, that it identifies five key visible aspects of this tradition equally intelligible to children, adolescents, and adults (God, Jesus, Bible, prayer, and church), and that the construct is operationalised through 24 Likert-type items arranged for scoring on a five-point scale: agree strongly, agree, not certain, disagree, and disagree strongly. The translation of this construct into other religious traditions involved proper theological awareness of the subtlety, complexity and diversity within these traditions.

The first of these instruments to be published was the Sahin-Francis Scale of Attitude toward Islam (Sahin & Francis, 2002). The items of the Francis Scale of Attitude toward Christianity were carefully scrutinised and debated by several Muslim scholars of Islam until agreement was reached on 23 Islam-related items which mapped closely onto the area assessed by the parent instrument.

The psychometric properties of the instrument were assessed on 381 Muslim adolescents in England (Sahin & Francis, 2002) and later confirmed among 1,199 Muslim adolescents in Kuwait (Francis, Sahin, & Al-Failakawi, 2008). Further work on the Sahin-Francis Scale of Attitude toward Islam is reported by Musharraf, Lewis, and Sultan (2014) among 174 students in Pakistan, by Hamid, Robbins, Nadeem, and Khan (2016) among 729 students in Pakistan, and by Francis, Tekke, and Robbins (2016) among 189 students in Malaysia.

The second of these instruments was the Katz-Francis Scale of Attitude toward Judaism (Francis & Katz, 2007). A similar process involving Jewish scholars of Judaism reached agreement on 24 Judaism-related items which mapped closely onto the area assessed by the parent instrument. The psychometric properties of the instrument were assessed on 618 Hebrew-speaking undergraduate students attending Bar-Ilan University, and later confirmed by Yablon, Francis, and Robbins (2014) on a further sample of 884 students in Israel, and by Lumbroso, Fayn, Tiliopoulos, and Francis (2016) among 101 Australian Jews.

The third of these instruments was the Santosh-Francis Scale of Attitude toward Hinduism (Francis, Santosh, Robbins, & Vij, 2008). A similar process involving Hindu scholars of Hinduism reached agreement on 19 Hinduism-related items which mapped closely onto the area assessed by the parent instrument. The psychometric properties of the instrument were assessed on 330 young Hindus in England (Francis, Santosh, Robbins, & Vij, 2008), and later confirmed among 100 Hindus in India (Tiliopoulos, Francis, & Slattery, 2010), among 309 Balinese Hindus (Lesmana, Tiliopoulos, & Francis, 2011), and among 149 Hindu students in India (Francis, Kamble, & Robbins, 2016).

The fourth and most recent of these instruments was the Athwal-Francis Scale of Attitude toward Sikhism (Francis, Athwal, & McKenna, under review). A similar process involving Sikh scholars identified a pool of 30 items proposed to reflect within this religious tradition the underlying attitudinal construct assessed by the parent instrument. Drawing on data provided by 90 self-assigned Sikh students in England between the ages of 13 and 15 years, factor analysis and reliability analysis were employed to select the 24 items with the best psychometric properties.

Providing that the underlying construct is operationalised in similar ways by similar instruments grounded in different faith traditions, it is reasonable to set the findings of these different instruments side by side. However, Astley, Francis, and Robbins (2012) proposed a different solution to the same problem. In the development of the Astley-Francis Scale of Attitude toward Theistic Faith, they suggested that a single set of items should make it possible to access the attitudinal dimension of religion across the major theistic faith traditions. Building on the short seven-item form of the Francis Scale of Attitude toward Christianity, Astley, Francis, and Robbins (2012) identified seven items concerned with affective responses to God, places of worship, and prayer that they regarded as conceptually appropriate within a Christian context, an Islamic context, and a post-Christian context. The psychometric properties of the new instrument were established on a sample of 284 16- to 18-year-old students in England, and later confirmed by Francis, Brockett, and Village (2013) on a sample of 4,353 students from England between the ages of 11 and 16 years, by Francis and Lewis (2016a) among a sample of 10,678 students from the four nations of the UK between the ages of 13 and 15 years, and by Francis and Crea (under review) among a sample of 934 Italian-speaking participants between the ages of 13 and 80 years.

3 Personality and Religion

When Argyle (1958) undertook his first systematic review of empirical research within the psychology of religion, he concluded that insufficient consistent research had been thus far undertaken to establish reliable findings regarding the connection between personality and religion. Forty years later when Beit-Hallahmi and Argyle (1997, p. 164) re-examined the literature they concluded that, by that stage, there was enough secure empirical evidence to locate individual differences in religiosity within an established model of personality. The model that they identified was the dimensional model of personality proposed by the Eysenckian family of personality measures. In the earlier form of the Eysenck Personality Inventory (Eysenck & Eysenck, 1964) this model comprised two dimensions, namely extraversion and neuroticism. In the later forms of the Eysenck Personality Questionnaire (Eysenck & Eysenck, 1975) and of the Eysenck Personality Questionnaire Revised (Eysenck, Eysenck, & Barrett, 1985) this model comprised three dimensions, namely extraversion, neuroticism, and psychoticism. The shift that Beit-Hallahmi and Argyle (1997) identified was documented by a series of studies employing the Francis Scale of Attitude toward Christianity. Three main conclusions emerge from these studies.

The first conclusion concerns the relationship between attitude toward Christianity and neuroticism scores. Eysenck and Eysenck (1975) defined high scorers on the neuroticism scale as being anxious, worrying, moody, and frequently depressed individuals who are likely to sleep badly and to suffer from various psychosomatic disorders. They are seen as overly emotional, reacting too strongly to all sorts of stimuli, and finding it difficult to get back on an even keel after emotionally arousing experiences. Strong reactions interfere with their proper adjustment, making them react in irrational, sometimes rigid ways. Highly neurotic individuals are worriers whose main characteristic is a constant preoccupation with things that might go wrong, and a strong anxiety reaction to these thoughts. After controlling for the expected sex differences, according to which females score more highly than males on both indices of religiosity (Argyle & Beit-Hallahmi, 1975) and neuroticism (Jorm, 1987), repeated analyses demonstrate no significant relationship between neuroticism scores and a positive attitude toward Christianity (Francis, Pearson, Carter, & Kay, 1981a; Francis, Pearson, & Kay, 1983a; Francis & Pearson, 1991).

The second conclusion concerns the relationship between attitude toward Christianity and psychoticism scores. Eysenck and Eysenck (1976) define high scorers on the psychoticism scale as being cold, impersonal, hostile, lacking in sympathy, unfriendly, untrustful, odd, unemotional, unhelpful, lacking in insight, and strange, with paranoid ideas that people are against them. Eysenck and Eysenck (1976) also use the following descriptors: egocentric, self-centered, impersonal, lacking in empathy, solitary, troublesome, cruel, glacial, inhumane, insensitive, sensation-seeking, aggressive, foolhardy, enjoy making fools of others, and liking odd and unusual things. Eysenck and Eysenck (1975) maintained that emotions such as empathy and guilt are characteristically absent in people who score high on measures of psychoticism. Repeated analyses demonstrate a significant negative relationship between psychoticism scores and a positive attitude toward Christianity (Kay, 1981a; Francis & Pearson, 1985a; Francis, 1992c).

The third conclusion concerns the relationship between attitude toward Christianity and extraversion scores. Originally Eysenck defined high scorers on the extraversion scale as sociable, outgoing, impulsive, carefree, and optimistic. This definition clearly combines the two notions of sociability and impulsivity (Eysenck & Eysenck, 1963). While both of these two components appear to have been well represented in the earlier editions of the extraversion scale, the subsequent editions have been largely purified of impulsivity, which now relates more closely to psychoticism (Rocklin & Revelle, 1981). While according to the earlier operationalisations of extraversion, introverts emerge as holding a more positive attitude toward Christianity, according to the later operationalisations repeated analyses demonstrate no significant relationship between extraversion scores and attitude toward Christianity (Francis, Pearson, Carter, & Kay, 1981b; Francis, Pearson, & Kay, 1983b; Francis & Pearson, 1985b; Williams, Robbins, & Francis, 2005).

The consensus of these focused analyses is given further support by studies conducted among other samples of school students in the United Kingdom, using the Francis Scale of Attitude toward Christianity, including

8- to 11-year-old students (Robbins, Francis, & Gibbs, 1995), 11-year-old students (Francis, Lankshear, & Pearson, 1989), 12- to 16-year-old students (Francis & Montgomery, 1992; Williams, Robbins, & Francis, 2006), 15- to 16-year-old students (Francis & Pearson, 1988), and 16- to 18-year-old students (Wilcox & Francis, 1997; Francis & Fearn, 1999; Fearn, Lewis, & Francis, 2003). The findings have also been replicated among secondary school students in Germany (Francis & Kwiran, 1999b).

Another set of studies has employed the Francis Scale of Attitude toward Christianity alongside the Eysenck measures of personality among university students and adults, including studies in the United Kingdom (Francis, 1991a, 1993b; Francis & Bennett, 1992; Carter, Kay, & Francis, 1996; Bourke & Francis, 2000; Shuter-Dyson, 2000; Bourke, Francis, & Robbins, 2005; Williams & Francis, 2006; Williams, Robbins, & Francis, 2006), Australia and Canada (Francis, Lewis, Brown, Philipchalk, & Lester, 1995), Northern Ireland (Lewis & Joseph, 1994; Lewis, 1999, 2000), Republic of Ireland (Maltby, 1997a; Maltby & Lewis, 1997), the USA (Lewis & Maltby, 1995b; Roman & Lester, 1999), France (Lewis & Francis, 2000, 2014), Greece (Youtika, Joseph, & Diduca, 1999), Hong Kong (Francis, Lewis, & Ng, 2003), and South Africa (Francis & Kerr, 2003). Once again, the basic pattern was confirmed that attitude toward Christianity was negatively correlated with psychoticism, but unrelated to either extraversion or neuroticism. Moreover, other studies have reported similar results using the Katz-Francis Scale of Attitude toward Judaism (Francis, Katz, Yablon, & Robbins, 2004) and the Santosh-Francis Scale of Attitude toward Hinduism (Francis, Robbins, Santosh, & Bhanot, 2008).

Being purely cross-sectional correlational studies, the data currently available are not able to adjudicate on the direction of causality in the relationship reported. Eysenck's psychologically driven theory would argue for the priority of personality in shaping these relationships, seeing individual differences in personality to be biologically based. According to this account, individuals who record low scores on the psychoticism scale would be more drawn to the Christian tradition. Such a view is consistent with Eysenck's notion regarding the relationship between low psychoticism and greater conditioning into tenderminded social attitudes and the general location of religiosity within the domain of tenderminded social attitudes (Eysenck, 1975, 1976). On the other hand, such a psychologically driven theory may be hard-pressed to explain the lack of relationship between neuroticism scores and religion, since the psychological mechanism posited here suggests that religion provides an attractive escape for neurotic anxieties.

An alternative theologically driven theory would argue for the priority of religious experience in shaping the relationship between personality, mental health, and religion, seeing religion as essentially transformative of individual differences. According to this account, individuals who record high scores on the Francis Scale of Attitude toward Christianity would be challenged by their faith to transform and reject those qualities listed by Eysenck as characterising the high scorer on the psychoticism scale: egocentric, self-centred, impersonal, lacking in empathy, solitary, troublesome, cruel, glacial, inhumane, insensitive, sensation-seeking, aggressive, and foolhardy (Eysenck & Eysenck, 1976). On the other hand, such theologically driven theory may be more hard-pressed to account for the lack of association between attitude toward Christianity and neuroticism. Throughout the Gospel tradition the Christian faith consistently proclaims the twin messages of 'Fear not' and 'Peace be with you' from the angelic annunciation preceding the Lucan birth narrative to the Johannine post-resurrection appearances. According to such theory the Christian disciple should be less troubled by those qualities listed by Eysenck as characterising the high scorer on the neuroticism scale: anxious, worrying, moody, frequently depressed, poor sleepers, suffering from various psychosomatic disorders, and overly emotional (Eysenck & Eysenck, 1975).

While the Eysenckian model of personality speaks in terms of three major dimensions (extraversion, neuroticism, and psychoticism), an alternative model of personality, as promoted by Costa and McCrae (1992) through the Revised NEO Personality Inventory (NEO, PI-R) and the NEO Five-Factor Inventory (NEO-FFI), discusses individual differences in terms of five domains characterised as neuroticism, extraversion, openness, agreeableness, and conscientiousness. Although an increasingly influential model in personality psychology, Saroglou (2002) observed that the model had been slow to make an impact within the psychology of religion and was able to identify only 13 studies as suitable for inclusion in his meta-analytic review of evidence relating religion and the five factors of personality. This meta-analytic review concluded that different measures of religiosity related to the five personality factors in different ways and that, overall, the effect sizes were small.

In a subsequent paper, Saroglou and Muñoz-Garcia (2008) speculated about how a religious person might respond differently from a non-religious person:

> [W]hen facing stress and emotions ('neuroticism'), novelty ('openness to experience'), challenges from internal and external world that ask for self-control, orderliness, and responsibility ('conscientiousness'), when s/he is invested in interpersonal relationships ('agreeableness'), or is in contact and functions with others in general and in groups ('extraversion').
> SAROGLOU AND MUÑOZ-GARCIA, 2008, p. 84

PSYCHOLOGICAL PERSPECTIVES ON RELIGIOUS EDUCATION

Such global generalisations about the association between personality and religion may need to be nuanced in the light of the kind of differentiations made by theories of religious orientation, as well as in light of the findings of the earlier meta-analytic review.

The best-established conceptualisation of religious orientations, as proposed originally by Allport and Ross (1967) and extended subsequently by Batson and Ventis (1982), distinguishes between three ways of being religious or three religious motivations characterised as intrinsic religiosity, extrinsic religiosity, and quest religiosity (Francis, 2007). Straightforward studies that have run recognised measures of these religious orientations alongside the five-factor model of personality remain scarce.

In an early study, Taylor and MacDonald (1999) employed the two measures of intrinsic religiosity (nine items) and extrinsic religiosity (11 items) proposed by Allport and Ross (1967) among a sample of 368 university students. According to these data, intrinsic religiosity was associated with higher agreeableness scores ($r = .25$), and higher conscientiousness scores ($r = .23$), while extrinsic religiosity was associated with higher neuroticism scores ($r = .11$), and lower openness scores ($r = .18$).

In another early study, Kosek (1999) employed the Polish version of the Swedish Religious Orientations Scale proposed by Hovemyr (1998), assessing intrinsic religiosity (10 items), extrinsic religiosity (12 items), and quest religiosity (6 items), among a sample of 104 school students aged around 14 years. According to these data, intrinsic religiosity was associated with higher agreeableness scores ($r = .41$) and higher conscientiousness scores ($r = .50$), extrinsic religiosity was associated with higher extraversion scores ($r = .21$), and quest religiosity was associated with higher agreeableness ($r = .26$) scores and higher conscientiousness scores ($r = .28$).

In a later study, Robbins, Francis, McIlroy, Clarke, and Pritchard (2010) employed the measures of intrinsic religiosity (9 items) and extrinsic religiosity (11 items) proposed by Allport and Ross (1967) and the measure of quest religiosity (12 items) proposed by Batson and Schoenrade (1991a, 1991b) alongside the Big Five Factor model of personality proposed by Costa and McCrae (1992). In this study, Robbins, Francis, McIlroy, Clarke, and Pritchard (2010) assessed the five factors by Goldberg's lexicon approach to personality assessment (Goldberg, 1990, 1992). Each of the five factors was assessed by five five-point semantic differential grids. Openness was assessed by: imaginative versus unimaginative, creative versus uncreative, curious versus uninquisitive, reflective versus unreflective, sophisticated versus unsophisticated. Conscientiousness was assessed by: organised versus disorganised, responsible versus irresponsible, practical versus impractical, thorough versus careless, hardworking versus lazy. Extraversion was assessed by: talkative versus silent, assertive versus unassertive, adventurous versus unadventurous, energetic versus unenergetic, bold versus timid. Agreeableness was assessed by: kind versus unkind, cooperative versus uncooperative, unselfish versus selfish, trustful versus distrustful, generous versus stingy. Neuroticism was assessed by: tense versus relaxed, nervous versus at ease, unstable versus stable, discontented versus contented, emotional versus unemotional. The data demonstrated that individual differences in the three religious orientations were largely independent of the five personality factors, with the exception of significant positive correlation between intrinsic religiosity and agreeableness. These findings support Piedmont's (1999) contention that religiosity is largely independent of personality when personality is operationalised in terms of the Big Five Factors.

4 Sex Differences in Religion

Sex differences are among the most obvious differences observed by an individual differences approach to psychology. In their classic review of empirical research in the social psychology of religion, Argyle and Beit-Hallahmi (1975) concluded that:

> The differences between men and women in their religious behaviour and beliefs are considerable ... This is one of the most important of the statistical comparisons to be made in this book.
>
> ARGYLE AND BEIT-HALLAHMI, 1975, p. 71

Two decades later, Francis (1997) confirmed Argyle and Beit-Hallahmi's assessment of the existing literature. More recent empirical evidence generated from a Christian (or post-Christian) context during the twenty-first century continues to indicate that women are more religious than men. The empirical evidence in terms of gender differences in church attendance is consistent across many different locations, including: Africa (Akinyele & Akinyele, 2007), Australia (Moxy, McEvoy, & Bowe, 2011), Canada and the USA (Maselko & Kubzansky, 2006; Eagle, 2011), and Western Europe (Crockett & Voas, 2006; Pollak & Pickel, 2007). The empirical evidence for women being more religious than men within a Christian context is consistent across a range of other indicators of religiosity in addition to church attendance, including: attitude toward religion (Francis, Ispas, Robbins, Ilie, & Iliescu, 2009), denominational membership (Smith, Denton, Faris, & Regenerus, 2002), religious belief

PSYCHOLOGICAL PERSPECTIVES ON RELIGIOUS EDUCATION

(Bartkowski & Hempel, 2009), religious experience and spiritual connection with God (Baker, 2008; Anthony, Hermans, & Sherkat, 2010). While, the empirical evidence supporting the claim that women are more religious than men has remained stable from the time of Argyle and Beit-Hallahmi's (1975) classic review to the end of the second decade of the twenty-first century, considerable change has taken place in the weight given to different theories for explaining this difference between men and women.

Reviewing the body of empirical research concerned with sex differences in religion, Francis and Penny (2014) cautioned against unguarded generalisation of the view that women are more religious than men beyond the Christian and post-Christian contexts. They also documented the controversy concerning a satisfactory theoretical framework which can account for the observed differences. Broadly speaking, two main groups of theories have been advanced to account for the greater religiosity of women: sociologically grounded theories and psychologically grounded theories. Sociologically grounded theories are concerned with the external social and contextual factors that may help to shape the experiences of men and women differently. Psychologically grounded theories are concerned with the internal factors that may help to shape the way that individuals (both men and women) respond differently to experiences. In particular, the individual differences approach to sex differences in religion has drawn on gender-orientation theories.

Gender-orientation theories focus specifically on the psychological constructs of masculinity and femininity that are considered as stable and enduring aspects of personality among both men and women. Gender-orientation theory has its roots in the conceptualisation and measurement proposed by Bem (1981) through the Bem Sex Role Inventory. According to this conceptualisation, masculinity and femininity are not bipolar descriptions of a unidimensional construct, but two orthogonal personality dimensions. Empirically the Bem Sex Role Inventory demonstrates considerable variations in both femininity and masculinity among both men and women. This theory was brought into the debate on sex differences in religiosity by Thompson (1991), who argued that individual differences in religiosity should be affected more by gender-orientation than by being male or female. According to this approach, being religious is a consonant experience for *people* with a feminine orientation, while men as well as women can have a feminine orientation.

Thompson (1991) formulated two hypotheses concerning the relationship between gender-orientation and individual differences in religiosity between men and women. The first hypothesis was that, if being religious is a gender type attribute related to women's lives in general, then multivariate analyses which control for the personality dimensions of masculinity and femininity should demonstrate that being female continues to have a significant effect in predicting religiosity. The second hypothesis was that, if being religious is a function of gender-orientation, then multivariate analyses which control for the personality dimensions of masculinity and femininity should result in no additional variance being explained by being female. Thompson's analysis of data from a sample of undergraduate students in the USA, who completed the Bem Sex Role Inventory (Bem, 1981) alongside five measures of religiosity, supported the hypothesis that being religious is a function of gender-orientation.

Building on this research model, a series of studies have employed the Bem Sex Role Inventory (Bem, 1981) alongside the Francis Scale of Attitude toward Christianity (Francis, Lewis, Philipchalk, Brown, & Lester, 1995), to test Thompson's hypotheses. The findings from these studies, reported by Francis and Wilcox (1996, 1998) and by Francis (2005a), have demonstrated that femininity scores predict gender differences in religiosity. Most important, however, is the finding that, when these studies employed multiple-regression to control for the impact of gender-orientation on religiosity, sex had no additional impact on individual differences in religiosity. This demonstrates, in agreement with Thompson's hypotheses, that higher levels of religiosity may be interpreted as a function of gender-orientation rather than as a function of being female. Other empirical studies utilising alternative measures of religiosity alongside the Bem Sex Role Inventory (Bem, 1981) support the conclusion that higher femininity scores are associated with higher levels of religiosity within the context of the Christian faith (Smith, 1990; Mercer & Durham, 1999) and within the context of the Islamic faith (Abu-Ali & Reisen, 1999), although these studies do not proceed to explore whether or not biological sex accounts for further variance in religiosity scores after controlling for femininity scores.

Recognising that the Bem Sex Role Inventory (Bem, 1981) is open to the criticism that conceptualisation of sex roles has changed considerably since this instrument was first validated, Penny, Francis, and Robins (2015) set out to test whether Thompson's (1991) hypothesis could be sustained by using other measures of psychological masculinity or psychological femininity. They argued that personality-based theories propose the existence of a range of stable and enduring psychological constructs that consistently differentiate between men and women. Such constructs, Penny, Francis, and Robbins (2015) argued, could be employed in regression models in the same way that Thompson (1991) employed the Bem Sex Role Inventory. In particular they drew attention to the three-dimensional model of personality proposed by Eysenck (Eysenck & Eysenck, 1991), and operationalized through the

PSYCHOLOGICAL PERSPECTIVES ON RELIGIOUS EDUCATION 23

Eysenck Personality Questionnaire (Eysenck & Eysenck, 1975) and the Eysenck Personality Questionnaire Revised (Eysenck, Eysenck, & Barrett, 1985). This model maintains that individual differences can be most adequately and economically summarised in terms of the three higher-order factors defined by the high scoring poles as extraversion, neuroticism, and psychoticism. Two of these factors have recorded significant and stable sex differences over time and across cultures. From the early development of the three-dimensional model, higher psychoticism scores were associated with being male (Eysenck & Eysenck, 1976), on a continuum from tendermindedness, through tough-mindedness, to psychotic disorder. Indeed, in their identification of seven constituent components of high psychoticism scores, Eysenck, Barrett, Wilson, and Jackson (1992) label one of these components as masculinity. On the other hand, higher neuroticism scores have been associated with being female (see Francis, 1993c), on a continuum from emotional stability, through emotional lability, to neurotic disorder.

A series of studies employing Eysenck's dimensional model of personality alongside the Francis Scale of Attitude toward Christianity (Francis, Lewis, Philipchalk, Brown, & Lester, 1995) has demonstrated that psychoticism scores comprise the dimension of personality fundamental to individual differences in religiosity, and that neuroticism scores are unrelated to individual differences in religiosity after controlling for sex differences (Kay, 1981a; Francis & Pearson, 1985a; Francis, 1992c). These findings have been consistently replicated internationally, including in: Australia and Canada (Francis, Lewis, Brown, Philipchalk, & Lester, 1995), Northern Ireland (Lewis & Joseph, 1994; Lewis, 1999, 2000), Republic of Ireland (Maltby, 1997a), the USA (Roman & Lester, 1999), France (Lewis & Francis, 2000), Greece (Youtika, Joseph, & Diduca, 1999), Hong Kong (Francis, Lewis, & Ng, 2003), and South Africa (Francis & Kerr, 2003), as well as in the UK (Francis, 1999). Moreover, later studies have reported similar results within the context of the Jewish faith (Francis, Katz, Yablon, & Robbins, 2004), and the Hindu faith (Francis, Robbins, Santosh, & Bhanot, 2008). These findings would account for sex differences in religiosity in terms of basic differences between men and women in levels of psychoticism.

Further support for this view, drawing on Eysenck's three dimensional model of personality, is provided by a series of studies exploring the personality profile of male clergy. Routinely these studies have suggested that male clergy display a characteristically feminine profile in terms of recording low scores on the psychoticism scale (see Francis, 1991b, 1992e; Robbins, Francis, & Rutledge, 1997; Robbins, Francis, Haley, & Kay, 2001).

In order to test this theory, Penny, Francis, and Robbins (2015) administered the Francis Scale of Attitude toward Christianity (Francis, Lewis, Philipchalk,

Brown, & Lester, 1995), and measures of frequency of worship attendance and frequency of personal prayer, together with the short form of the Eysenck Personality Questionnaire Revised (Eysenck, Eysenck, & Barrett, 1985), to a sample of 1,682 undergraduate students in Wales. The sample comprised 443 males (26%), 1,235 females (73%), and 4 respondents who failed to disclose their sex; 1,204 were aged under 20 (72%), 349 were aged between 20 and 29 (21%), 86 were aged between 30 and 39 (5%), 37 were aged between 40 and 49 (2%), and 6 respondents failed to disclose their age. Within this sample, 18% claimed they went to church weekly, and 23% claimed they never went to church; 15% claimed that they prayed daily, and 24% claimed that they never prayed.

Penny, Francis, and Robbins (2015) analysed the data generated by this study in two steps. In the first step they examined the bivariate correlations between personality, religion and sex. Two features of the correlation matrix merit comment. First, these data demonstrate that there is a significant positive correlation between sex and all three measures of religiosity. Females record higher frequency of church attendance, higher frequency of personal prayer, and a more positive attitude toward Christianity than males. Second, these data demonstrate: a significant negative correlation between psychoticism and church attendance, personal prayer, and attitude toward Christianity. In the second step they generated three regression models which propose church attendance, personal prayer, and attitude toward Christianity as the dependent variables and which examine the cumulative predictive power of personality and sex, entered in that fixed-order. These data confirm that psychoticism is the key predictor of religiosity in respect of church attendance, personal prayer, and attitude toward Christianity. These data also demonstrate that, after controlling for all personality dimensions in each model, sex contributes no additional predictive power to church attendance, personal prayer, or attitude toward Christianity. In conclusion this study conducted among undergraduates in Wales confirms that within Christian or post-Christian contexts women are still found to be more religious than men, and that greater religiosity among women can be adequately accounted for in terms of basic personality differences.

5   Correlates of Religious Affect

When the Francis Scale of Attitude toward Christianity was first published, Francis (1978a, 1978b) invited colleagues to collaborate in developing a network of studies that could generate a composite picture of the correlates of individual differences in religious affect that agreed on this common measure. In the following forty years a significant body of knowledge has been built up using the Francis Scale of Attitude toward Christianity and helpfully complemented and augmented by studies employing the wider family of instruments, including the Sahin-Francis Scale of Attitude toward Islam, the Katz-Francis Scale of Attitude toward Judaism, the Santosh-Francis Scale of Attitude toward Hinduism, and the Astley-Francis Scale of Attitude toward Theistic Faith.

For example, one group of studies has consistently worked with the Oxford Happiness Inventory developed by Argyle, Martin, and Crossland (1989) to assess the consistency with which there may be a correlation between religious affect and personal wellbeing. In their foundation study, Robbins and Francis (1996) administered the Francis Scale of Attitude toward Christianity and the Oxford Happiness Inventory among a sample of 360 first-year undergraduate students in Wales. This study reported a significant positive correlation between religious affect and personal happiness. Subsequently seven other studies were published that confirmed the finding from the original study. These studies draw on the following samples: 212 undergraduate students in the United States of America (Francis & Lester, 1997); 295 individuals, ranging in age from late teens to late seventies, recruited from participants attending a variety of courses and workshops on the psychology of religion (Francis & Robbins, 2000); 994 15- to 16-year-old secondary school students (Francis, Jones, & Wilcox, 2000); 496 members of the University of the Third Age (Francis, Jones, & Wilcox, 2000); 456 undergraduate students in Wales (Francis, Jones, & Wilcox, 2000); 89 students in Wales (Francis, Robbins, & White, 2003), and 3,848 sixth-form students in the Republic of Ireland (Francis & Lewis, 2016b).

Taken together these eight samples (N = 360, 212, 295, 994, 496, 456, 89, 3,848) demonstrated a consistent pattern of a significant positive correlation between religion and happiness based on employing the same instruments in different contexts. The scientific strategy of replication seemed to be bearing fruit, although further replication studies remain desirable. On the other hand, two further replication studies failed to find this positive association between scores recorded on the Francis Scale of Attitude toward Christianity, using the German translation of the Oxford Happiness Inventory among 331 students (Francis, Ziebertz, & Lewis, 2003), and using the Estonian translation of the Oxford Happiness Measure among 150 students (Francis, Elken, & Robbins, 2012).

Subsequently, working within other faith traditions, the Oxford Happiness Inventory has been administered alongside the Katz-Francis Scale of Attitude toward Judaism (Francis & Katz, 2007) in three studies in Israel reported by

Francis and Katz (2002) among 298 female students, Francis, Katz, Yablon, and Robbins (2004) among 203 male students, and Francis, Yablon, and Robbins (2014) among 348 female students. The Oxford Happiness Inventory has been administered alongside the Ok Religious Attitude Scale (Islam) (Ok, 2016), by Francis, Ok, and Robbins (2017) among 348 students in Turkey, and alongside the Sahin-Francis Scale of Attitude toward Islam (Sahin & Francis, 2002) by Tekke, Francis, and Robbins (2018) among 189 students in Malaysia. The Oxford Happiness Inventory has been administered alongside the Santosh-Francis Scale of Attitude toward Hinduism (Francis, Santosh, Robbins, & Vij, 2008) by Tiliopoulos, Francis, and Slattery (2011) among 100 Hindu affiliates from the Bunt caste in South India. All six studies reported a positive significant correlation between these measures of religious affect and scores recorded on the Oxford Happiness Inventory.

Another group of studies has consistently explored the relationship between the attitudinal dimension of religion, attitude toward science, scientism, and creationism among young people in Kenya (Fulljames & Francis, 1987b; Fulljames & Francis, 2003), Scotland (Gibson, 1989b; Francis, Gibson, & Fulljames, 1990; Fulljames, Gibson, & Francis, 1991; Francis, Fulljames, & Gibson, 1992), England (Fulljames, 1996; Astley & Francis, 2010); Northern Ireland (Francis & Greer, 2001), and throughout the United Kingdom (Francis, Astley, & McKenna, 2018, 2019). These studies highlight the ways in which both scientism and creationism can inhibit the development of positive attitudes toward *both* science *and* Christianity.

This stream of research has involved the operationalisation of a family of constructs variously described as 'an exaggerated belief in science', 'scientism', and 'scientific fundamentalism'. The first instrument of this series, Fulljames' scale measuring an exaggerated belief in science, as reported by Fulljames, Gibson, and Francis (1991) and by Francis and Greer (2001), comprised the following five items:
- Science will eventually give us complete control over the world.
- Theories in science can be proved to be definitely true.
- The laws of science will never be changed.
- Theories in science are never proved with absolute certainty (reverse coded).
- Nothing should be believed unless it can be proved scientifically.

The internal consistency reliability of this instrument was, however, quite poor. Among a sample of 729 16- to 18-year-old students in Scotland, Fulljames, Gibson, and Francis (1991) reported an alpha coefficient of .56. Among a sample of 1,584 14- to 16-year-old students in Northern Ireland, Francis and Greer (2001) reported an alpha coefficient of .54.

In order to improve on Fulljames' measure, Astley and Francis (2010) proposed a seven-item scale (which they named as a measure of scientism), adding the following two items to Fulljames' original five items:
- Science can give us absolute truths.
- Science alone can provide truths about nature.

Among a sample of 187 female sixth-form students, Astley and Francis (2010) reported an alpha coefficient of .77. Subsequently, in order to provide a shorter reliable measure, Francis, Astley, and McKenna (2019) proposed a three-item scale (which they renamed as a measure of scientific fundamentalism), comprising the following items from the seven-item scale:
- Theories in science can be proved to be definitely true.
- The laws of science will never be changed.
- Science can give us absolute truths.

Among a sample of nearly 11,809 13- to 15-year-old students, Francis, Astley, and McKenna (2019) reported an alpha coefficient of .69. This three-item scale was also used by Francis, Astley, and McKenna (2018).

In an independent strand of research, Farias, Newheiser, Kahane, and de Toledo (2013) proposed a ten-item scale of belief in science that comprised the following items:
- Science provides us with a better understanding of the universe than does religion.
- 'In a demon-haunted world, science is a candle in the dark.' (Carl Sagan)
- We can only rationally believe in what is scientifically provable.
- Science tells us everything there is to know about what reality consists of.
- All the tasks human beings face are soluble by science.
- The scientific method is the only reliable path to knowledge.
- The only real kind of knowledge we can have is scientific knowledge.
- Science is the most valuable part of human culture.
- Science is the most efficient means of attaining truth.
- Scientists and science should be given more respect in modern society.

Among a sample of 144 rowers, Farias, Newheiser, Kahane, and de Toledo (2013) reported an alpha coefficient of .86. In a subsequent study among 373 Iranian students, Aghababaei (2016) reported an alpha coefficient of .87 for the Persian translation of the instrument.

In a recent study within this stream, Francis, Astley, and McKenna (2018) drew on Edward Bailey's theory of implicit religion (see Bailey, 1997, 1998, 2002) to explore the implications of scientific fundamentalism as implicit religion. These data suggested that scientific fundamentalism could serve functions in people's lives similar to those served by explicit religion. Such reconceptualization of scientific fundamentalism as implicit religion then enabled the conflict between scientific fundamentalism and religion to be reconceptualised in terms of the theology of religions, in which the exclusivist position shows little tolerance for other belief systems.

Other research within this tradition examining the correlates of the attitudinal dimension of religion can best be introduced within two main themes. The first main theme has explored the relationship between the attitudinal dimension of religion and other key major personality-related constructs. These constructs include abortion-related attitudes (Fawcett, Andrews, & Lester, 2000), adjustment (Schludermann, Schludermann, Needham, & Mulenga, 2001), alcohol-related attitudes (Francis, Fearn, & Lewis, 2005), altruism (Eckert & Lester, 1997), Cattell's personality model (Francis & Bourke, 2003; Bourke, Francis, & Robbins, 2007), dissociation (Dorahy & Lewis, 2001), conservatism (Lewis & Maltby, 2000), dogmatism (Francis, 2001; Francis & Robbins, 2003), empathy (Francis & Pearson, 1987), gender orientation (Francis & Wilcox, 1996, 1998; Francis, 2005a), general health (Francis, Robbins, Lewis, Quigley, & Wheeler, 2004), impulsivity (Pearson, Francis, & Lightbown, 1986), intelligence (Francis, 1998), intrinsic and extrinsic religiosity (Joseph & Lewis, 1997; Maltby & Day, 1998), just world beliefs (Crozier & Joseph, 1997), life satisfaction (Lewis, Joseph, & Noble, 1996; Lewis, 1998), mental health values (Tjeltveit, Fiordalisi, & Smith, 1996), moral values (Francis & Greer, 1990b), obsessionality (Lewis, 1994, 1996; Lewis & Joseph, 1994, Lewis & Maltby, 1994, 1995c; Maltby, 1997b; Maltby, McCollam, & Millar, 1994), openness to members of other religious traditions (Greer, 1985), operational thinking (Kay, Francis, & Gibson, 1996), paranormal belief (Williams, Francis, & Robbins, 2006), premarital sex (Francis, 2006), preoedipal fixation (Lewis & Maltby, 1992), Jungian psychological type (Jones & Francis, 1999; Fearn, Francis, & Wilcox, 2001), prosocial values (Schludermann, Schludermann, & Huynh, 2000), psychological health (Francis & Hermans, 2009), psychological wellbeing (Francis, Jones, & Wilcox, 1997; Francis, Hills, Schludermann, & Schludermann, 2008), religious orientation (Maltby & Lewis, 1996; Jones, 1997), schizotypal traits (White, Joseph, & Neil, 1995; Diduca & Joseph, 1997; Joseph & Diduca, 2001), self-esteem (Jones & Francis, 1996; Penny & Francis, 2014), social desirability (Gillings & Joseph, 1996), suicidal ideation (Lester & Francis, 1993), and wellbeing (Halama, Martos, & Adamovová, 2010).

The second main theme has explored the social and contextual factors associated with the development of a positive attitude toward religion. Separate studies have focused on such factors as the possible influences associated with age (Francis, 1989a), sex, church, home, and primary school (Swindells, Francis, & Robbins, 2010), conversion experiences (Kay, 1981b), denominational identity (Francis, 1990; Greer & Francis, 1990; Maltby, 1995; Francis & Greer,

PSYCHOLOGICAL PERSPECTIVES ON RELIGIOUS EDUCATION 29

1999), generational changes (Francis, 1989b, 1989c, 1992d; Kay & Francis, 1996), parental church attendance (Francis & Gibson, 1993b), parental marital happiness (Kay, 1981c), religious education syllabuses (Kay, 1981d), religious experience (Greer & Francis, 1992; Francis & Greer, 1993; Francis, ap Siôn, Lewis, Robbins, & Barnes, 2006), social class (Francis, Pearson, & Lankshear, 1990; Gibson, Francis, & Pearson, 1990), Sunday school attendance (Francis, Gibson, & Lankshear, 1991) and television (Francis & Gibson, 1992, 1993a).

6   Church Schools, Households, and Religious Formation

The Francis Scale of Attitude toward Christianity has been employed in a series of studies to explore whether Anglican church schools in England and Wales may exert a distinctive influence on shaping students' attitudes toward Christianity. This question, however, needs to be set against a discussion of the history and rationale for Anglican schools within the state-maintained system of education in England and Wales.

The Church of England was clearly involved in creating the foundations for the current system of state-maintained education in England and Wales through establishing the National Society in 1811, long before the Education Act 1870 (Rich, 1970) established the mechanism to build state schools independently of voluntary initiatives. The history has been well rehearsed by Cruikshank (1963), Murphy (1971), Francis (1986a), and Chadwick (1997), among others. Within this history, a key contribution to shaping the present configuration of church schools in England and Wales was made by the Education Act 1944. Recognising the Church's difficulty in funding extensive post-war reconstruction of the educational system, the Education Act 1944 offered church schools a choice between two ways forward. The path of voluntary aided status allowed the Churches to retain basic control over key aspects of school management (including appointing a majority of governors, appointing core staff, and determining religious education provision), but at the cost of ongoing financial liability for the buildings. The path of voluntary controlled status allowed the churches to pass all ongoing financial liability to the public purse, while still owning the building and having reduced control over aspects of school management (Dent, 1947). While voluntary controlled schools were permitted to retain the denominational character of school worship, they were not permitted to offer denominational religious education (except by way of special provision for those parents who requested it). Voluntary controlled schools were to follow the religious education defined by the Local Agreed Syllabus in the same way as schools without a religious character.

The Church of England's *Vision for education*, published in the Autumn of 2016 (Church of England, 2016), carried the subtitle, *Deeply Christian, serving the common good*, a subtitle that neatly captured and succinctly re-expressed the classic affirmation of the Anglican Church's twin objectives within the state-maintained sector of schools as voiced by the Durham Report (1970). This report distinguished the general aim and the domestic aim. The general aim was defined in terms of the Church of England's service to the nation by providing community schools for the local neighbourhood. The domestic aim was defined in terms of providing a service for the Church.

In one sense, the notion of serving the common good can be conceptualised as 'deeply Christian'. In the language of the Durham Report (1970) the Church of England was in business to serve the nation (through its general aim in education) as a deeply Christian commitment to the education of all. In another sense, however, a 'deeply Christian' school may wish to share the good news of the Christian gospel in an explicit way (the domestic aim) as well as in an implicit way through service (the general aim). At points, the Church of England's vision for education offers some aspirations that may come quite close to sharing the good news of the Christian gospel. The executive summary of the Durham Report explains that:

> In Church schools the deeply Christian foundation for this vision will be seen explicitly in teaching and learning both in RE and across the curriculum and also in the authentically Christian worship and ethos of those schools.
> Church of England, 2016, p. 2

The conclusion explains that:

> We want pupils to leave schools with a rich experience and understanding of Christianity, and we are committed to offering them an encounter with Jesus Christ and with Christian faith and practice in a way which enhances their lives.
> Church of England, 2016, p. 13

It is claims of this nature that have rekindled a long-established research tradition focusing on assessing students' attitudes toward Christianity within church schools in England and Wales.

One strand of this research concerned with comparing students in Church of England and non-denominational state-maintained primary schools was initiated in 1974 and reported by Francis (1979b). Francis (1986b) compared attitude toward Christianity of year-five and year-six students attending ten Church of England voluntary-aided primary schools and fifteen non-denominational state-maintained schools in East Anglia in 1974, 1978, and again in 1982. After using multiple regression analysis to control for the influence of sex, age, parental church attendance, social class and IQ on students' attitudes toward Christianity, these data indicated that the Church of England schools exercised a small negative influence on their students' attitudes toward Christianity. The direction of the school influence on students' attitude was consistent for all three samples taken in 1974, 1978, and 1982. Then Francis (1987b) set out to replicate this earlier study among year-six students attending Church of England voluntary-aided, Church of England voluntary-controlled, and non-denominational state-maintained schools in Gloucestershire. These data attributed neither positive nor negative influence to Church of England voluntary-aided schools, but demonstrated a significant negative influence exercised by Church of England voluntary-controlled schools.

A second strand of this research was concerned with comparing students in Church of England and non-denominational state-maintained secondary schools. In the first study, Francis and Carter (1980) compared the attitude toward Christianity of year-eleven students attending Church of England voluntary-aided secondary schools and non-denominational state-maintained secondary schools in England. These data provided no support for the notion that Church of England secondary schools exert either a positive or a negative influence on their students' attitude toward religion. In the second study, Francis and Jewell (1992) compared the attitude toward the church of year-ten students attending the four non-denominational secondary schools and the one Church of England voluntary-controlled secondary school serving the area around the same town. The data demonstrated that the Church of England school recruited a higher proportion of students from churchgoing homes and that churchgoing homes tended to represent the higher social classes. After taking into account the influence of sex, social class, and parental religiosity, path analysis indicated that the Church of England school exerted neither a positive nor a negative influence on its students' religious practice, belief, or attitude.

A third (and recent) strand of this research was concerned with exploring whether aided status makes a difference within the primary sector for Anglican church schools. Francis, Lankshear, and Eccles (in press) report on the attitude toward Christianity of 4,581 year-four, year-five, and year-six students (8- to 11-years of age) attending 87 Church in Wales primary schools, and compare the responses of 1,678 students attending controlled schools with the responses of 2,903 students attending aided schools. After controlling for sex, age, and frequency of church attendance, voluntary aided status is associated with a more positive attitude toward Christianity. In other words, aided status does make a difference to the attitudinal dimension of students' religiosity.

A fourth (and recent) strand of this research was concerned with exploring how the admissions policies of Anglican secondary schools (either prioritising the general aim or the domestic aim) may impact the trajectory of students' attitudes toward Christianity. Francis and Village (in press) report on the attitude toward Christianity of 6,036 students (who self-identified as either Christian or no religion) in year-seven, year-eight, year-nine, year-ten, and year-eleven classes within ten Christian ethos secondary schools in England and Wales (eight Anglican, one joint Anglican and Catholic, and one operated by a Christian foundation). The data demonstrated the complex relationship between school admission policies, parental church attendance, and the student's age and sex. Church schools that admit a high proportion of students from churchgoing backgrounds recorded a significantly more positive attitude toward Christianity among their students.

The findings from the study reported by Francis and Village (in press) resonated strongly with the earlier findings reported by Francis and Gibson (1993b) who examined the connection between parental church attendance and both church attendance and attitude toward Christianity among their children. For this study, Francis and Gibson (1993b) draw on data provided by 3,414 11- to 12-year-old and 15- to 16-year-old students attending secondary schools in the city of Dundee, Scotland. Path analysis demonstrated clear evidence for the strong paths from parental church attendance to child church attendance and the strong paths from parental church attendance and child church attendance to student attitude toward Christianity.

The findings from the study reported by Francis and Village (in press) concerning the key role of parental influence in supporting both church attendance and a positive attitude toward Christianity also resonates with the conclusion of the report presented to the Church of England General Synod in February 2019 under the title *Growing faith: Churches, schools and households* (General Synod, 2019). This report states: 'research shows that parents have the largest influence on their children in matters of faith' (paragraph 11).

Evidence supporting this claim can be derived from several sources, including one stream of research that has been listening systematically to what young Anglicans themselves have to say about the relative importance of factors that sustain their church attendance. This stream of research has been influenced and shaped by the Australian National Church Life Survey, in which young churchgoers have been invited to complete a survey alongside the surveys completed by adult attenders. For example, in their report on the survey conducted among 10,101 10- to 14-year-old attenders within the 2001 Australian National Church Life Survey, Bellamy, Mou, and Castle (2005) found that parents have a central role in the development of faith. They concluded that the practice of family prayer times, the encouragement of a personal devotional life for children, and parents simply being prepared to talk with their children about faith are all aspects that are positively related to higher levels of belief and a more positive attitude toward and involvement in church life.

In their report on the survey conducted among 10,153 8- to 14-year-old church attenders within the 2001 Church Life Survey designed primarily for use in England (Churches Information for Mission, 2001), Francis and Craig (2006) drew attention to two key findings. The first finding is that having friends attending the same church is important to young people within this age group. The second finding is that parents play a crucial role through what they do and what they model outside their pattern of church attendance. The maintenance of a positive attitude toward church among 8- to 14-year-old church attenders is associated with having parents who support the faith in conversation and example at home.

In their report on the survey conducted among 6,252 8- to 14-year-old church attenders within the 2011 Australian National Church Life Survey, Francis, Penny, and Powell (2018) found that these data confirmed the power of parental example on frequency of church attendance. Frequent attendance among young churchgoers occurred when *both* parents attended as well. The most positive attitude toward their church was found among young churchgoers who had the opportunity to talk about God with their parents and who did not feel that their parents made them go to church. Young churchgoers responded to parental encouragement better than to parental pressure. Although peer influence within the church did not make much contribution to frequency of attendance, it made a contribution to shaping positive attitude toward church.

Building on these three studies shaped by Bellamy, Mou, and Castle (2005), Francis and Craig (2006), and Francis, Penny, and Powell (2018), Francis (in press) drew on data collected within schools in England and Wales (half of the schools were church schools within the state-maintained sector and half were schools without a religious character within the state-maintained sector) to identify 13- to 15-year-old students who self-defined as Anglicans. This method allowed research to be undertaken among non-churchgoing Anglicans as well as among churchgoing Anglicans. From a total sample of 7,059 students, 645 identified themselves as Anglican (Church of England or Church in Wales), that is fewer than one in ten of the sample. This study employed multiple regression to take into account the effects of personal factors (sex and age) and psychological factors (extraversion, neuroticism, and psychoticism) before testing for the effects of peer-related factors and parental factors. These data demonstrated that young Anglicans who practise their Anglican identity by attending church did so primarily because their parents were Anglican churchgoers. Moreover, young Anglican churchgoers were most likely to keep going if their churchgoing parents also talked with them about their faith. Among this age group of Anglicans, peer support seemed insignificant in comparison with parental support.

In a subsequent study, Francis, Lankshear, Eccles, and McKenna (2019) replicated the analyses reported by Francis (in press) on two further samples of young Anglicans: 2,019 9- to 11-year-old students attending church primary schools in Wales, and 2,323 13- to 15-year-old students attending church secondary schools mainly in England. The data demonstrated that young Anglicans who practised their Anglican identity by attending church did so primarily because their parents were Anglican churchgoers. Moreover, young Anglican churchgoers were most likely to keep going to church if their churchgoing parents (especially mother) talked with them about their faith.

These consistent findings from empirical research regarding the primary agency of parents in the religious formation of the young within modern plural and secular societies add weight to the insight of Pope John Paul II (1981) in *Familiaris Consortio* (The Role of the Christian Family in the Modern World) who commented as follows:

> In our own time, in a world often alien and even hostile to faith, believing families are of primary importance as centres of living, radiant faith. For this reason, the Second Vatican Council, using an ancient expression, calls the family the Ecclesia domestica. It is in the bosom of the family that parents are 'by word and example ... the first heralds of the faith with regard to their children'.
>
> *Familiaris Consortio*, 1656

7 Attitude toward Religious Diversity

The quantitative strand to the Young People's Attitudes to Religious Diversity Project (see Arweck, 2017) was located within the individual differences tradition. The questionnaire that was completed by nearly 12,000 13- to 15-year-old students (recruited in schools from across the four nations of the UK and from London as a special case) was designed on the basis of three sources of theory: the individual differences approach as shaped within the psychology of religion; the individual differences approach as shaped within empirical theology; and the insights generated by the preceding qualitative strand of the project.

There were built into the quantitative strand core established and psychometrically tested instruments, including: the abbreviated form of the Junior Eysenck Personality Questionnaire Revised (JEPQR-A; Francis, 1996), the Rosenberg Self-Esteem Scale (Rosenberg, 1965), the empathy scale of the Junior Eysenck Impulsiveness Questionnaire (Eysenck, Easting, & Pearson, 1984), an instrument derived from the adult measure of emotional empathy proposed by Mehrabian and Epstein (1972), and the Astley-Francis Scale of Attitude toward Theistic Faith (Astley, Francis, & Robbins, 2012). Alongside these established measures, the quantitative strand of the project included a number of tested items that could form the basis of new psychometric measures. Among the new psychometrically tested instruments that evolved from the project are the following: the eleven-item Attitude toward Religious Diversity Index (ARDI; Francis, Croft, Pyke, & Robbins, 2012; Francis & Village, 2014; Francis, Village, Penny, & Neil, 2014), the six-item Outgroup Prejudice Scale (OPS; Francis & Village, 2015a); the Astley-Francis Theology of Religions Index (AFTRI; Astley & Francis, 2016), the thirteen-item Scale of Attitude toward Religious Diversity (SARDI; Francis, ap Siôn, McKenna, & Penny, 2017), the twelve-item Muslim Attitude toward Religious Diversity Index (MARDI; Francis & McKenna, 2017a), the ten-item Scale of Attitude toward Freedom of Religious Clothing and Symbols in School (SAFORCS; Francis & McKenna, 2017b; Francis, Village, McKenna, & Penny, 2018), the seven-item Experience of Victimisation Index (EVI; Francis & McKenna, 2018), the three-item Index of Rejection of Religion (IRR; Francis, Astley, & McKenna, 2019), the three-item Index of Scientific Fundamentalism (ISF; Francis, Astley, & McKenna, 2019), the four-item Index of Religious Fundamentalism (IRF; Francis, Astley, & McKenna, 2019), the eight-item Scale of Catholic Sectarian Attitudes (SOCSA; McKinney, Francis, & McKenna, 2019), the seven-item Scale of Anti-Muslim Attitude (SAMA; Francis & McKenna, 2019), the five-item Scale of Anti-Sikh Attitude (SASA; McKenna & Francis, under review a), and the five-item Scale of Anti-Jewish Attitude (SAJA; McKenna & Francis, under review b).

The aim of the quantitative strand of the Young People's Attitude to Religious Diversity Project was to obtain at least 2,000 responses from 13- to 15-year-old students within each of the five locations of England, Northern Ireland, Scotland, Wales, and London, with half of the participants drawn from schools with a religious character, and half from schools without a religious foundation. All told, 11,809 students participated in the project. Such a rich source of data has produced a number of focused studies, concentrating on specific research problems or specific locations (for an interim overview see ap Siôn, 2017).

In terms of illuminating specific locations, Francis, Penny, and McKenna (2017) examined the extent to which religious education contributed to the common good in England. Francis and Penny (2017) explored the personal and social significance of diverse religious affiliation in London. Francis, Penny, and Neil (2017) examined the diversity among young people growing up as Catholic in Scotland, distinguishing among three groups whom they characterised as practising Catholics, lapsed Catholics, and those sliding from practising into lapsed. Francis, Penny, and ap Siôn (2017) examined the contribution of schools with a religious character to community cohesion in Wales. Francis, Penny, and Barnes (2017) tested the 'worlds apart' thesis among students attending Catholic and Protestant schools in Northern Ireland.

In terms of understanding attitudes toward freedom of religion and freedom of religious clothing and symbols in school, Francis, Village, McKenna, and Penny (2018) explored the views of students who self-identified as either 'no religion' or as Christian. Their data demonstrated that the positive acceptance of religious clothing and symbols in school was related to personal factors (being female) to psychological factors (low psychoticism scores) and religious factors (especially prayer). Francis and McKenna (2017b) addressed the same question among Muslim students. Here they found the importance of theological factors alongside religious factors.

In terms of exploring the social effects of schools with a religious character, Francis and Village (2014) found that in England and Wales students attending church schools held neither a more positive nor a less positive attitude toward religious diversity. In Scotland, Francis, Village, Penny, and Neil (2014) found that students attending Catholic schools held a more positive attitude toward religious diversity compared with students attending schools without a religious foundation. Francis and Village (2015a) assessed outgroup prejudice among students attending Catholic and Protestant schools in Northern Ireland. After taking personal, psychological, and religious factors into account, they found that little variance in levels of outgroup prejudice could be attributed to the type of schools attended.

In terms of the effectiveness of religious education, Francis, ap Siôn, McKenna, and Penny (2017) found a small but significant association between taking religious education as an examination subject and a positive attitude toward religious diversity, after controlling for contextual, personal, psychological, and religious factors.

In terms of exploring the psychological correlates of unbelief, Francis, Penny, and Pyke (2013) compared attitudes toward religious diversity among theists, agnostics, and atheists. They found that atheists were less tolerant of the rights of religious people. Francis, ap Siôn, and Penny (2014) examined the connection between atheism and social cohesion in Wales. They found that religious belief promotes, rather than detracts from, social cohesion.

In terms of exploring the profile of those who identify as Christian without practising, Francis, Pyke, and Penny (2015) found that the attitudinal profile of nominal Christian students is distinct from that of religiously unaffiliated students and that the overall difference is the direction of the attitudinal profile of practising Christian students.

In terms of developing scientific insights within the psychology of religion, Francis, Croft, and Pyke (2012) examined the connection between God images and personal empathy, demonstrating that the image of God as a God of mercy is associated with higher empathy scores, while the image of God as a God of justice is associated with lower empathy scores. Francis, Lewis, and McKenna (2017) explored the connection between spirituality and empathy. They found a positive correlation between spirituality and empathy after controlling for personal and psychological factors. Francis, Astley, and McKenna (2019) explored the conflict between science and religion and found that young people who believe in science in an unqualified way (scientific fundamentalism) are more distrustful of religion.

In terms of exploring the identity and experience of young Muslims, Francis and McKenna (2017c) and McKenna and Francis (2019) explored the distinctive religious and social values of male and of female Muslims respectively. These data demonstrated that self-identification as Muslim encased a distinctive profile in terms both of religiosity and social values. Francis and McKenna (2017a) explored the effects of religious and of theological factors on shaping young Muslims' attitude to religious diversity. They found that taking into account Muslim students' theological identity is more important than taking into account their religious practice. Francis and McKenna (2018) explored the experience of victimisation among Muslim students. They found that one in four Muslim students reported being bullied because of their religion, and that those students who take their faith seriously through participating in worship attendance experience higher levels of victimisation.

Following on from the study by Francis and McKenna (2017a) into the experience of victimisation among Muslim students, Francis and McKenna (2019) repeated their analyses among Christian students, defining Christian students as those who both self-identified as Christian and also attended religious worship services at least six times a year apart from special services (like weddings). They found that one in seven Christian students reported being bullied because of their religion. Male and female Christian students were equally vulnerable to victimisation. Christian students who took their religion to heart as praying people were the most vulnerable.

In terms of exploring what keeps young Christians in the church, two separate analyses by Francis and Casson (2019) among Catholics and by Francis (in press) among Anglicans drew attention to the core influence of the home environment. The study by Francis and Casson (2019), among 2,146 self-identified young Catholics living in England, Scotland, and Wales, found that young Catholics who practise their Catholic identity by attending church do so largely because their parents are Catholic churchgoers. Moreover, young Catholic churchgoers are most likely to keep going if both mother *and* father are Catholic churchgoers. Among this age group of young Catholics both peer support and attending a church school are also significant, but account for little additional variance after taking parental churchgoing into account.

In terms of generating new insight into the perceived problem of sectarianism in Scotland, McKinney, Francis, and McKenna (2019) set out to address one of the gaps in knowledge, the attitude of Catholic school students. Drawing on the data provided by 797 participants in the Young People's Attitudes to Religious Diversity Project from schools in Scotland who self-identified as Roman Catholic, McKinney, Francis, and McKenna (2019) developed the eight-item Scale of Catholic Sectarian Attitudes. This instrument not only demonstrated that sectarian attitudes exist within the young Catholic community in Scotland, but that this attitude has possibly become part of a wider problem generated by the public visibility of religious diversity within an increasingly secular society. The analysis assessed the influence of five sets of factors on shaping individual differences in sectarian attitudes: personal factors (sex and age), psychological factors (extraversion, neuroticism, and psychoticism), religious factors (identity, belief, and practice), theological factors (exclusivism), and contextual factors (Catholic schools). Two findings of particular significance were that sectarian attitudes are higher among nominal Catholics than among practising Catholics.

When the Young People's Attitudes to Religious Diversity Project was originally conceptualised particular attention was given to the opportunity for operationalisation and testing the classic contact hypothesis. The contact hypothesis (or intergroup contact theory) proposes that changes in belief about or attitude toward particular groups may come about from direct contact with members of those groups. By bringing people from different backgrounds together and encouraging collaboration, prejudice may be reduced and more

PSYCHOLOGICAL PERSPECTIVES ON RELIGIOUS EDUCATION 39

positive attitudes toward the other result. The contact hypothesis was originally developed by Gordon Allport. Allport (1954) asserted that prejudice
arose because of negative assumptions made about entire groups of people.
He suggested that interpersonal contact between members of different groups,
if undertaken in appropriate situations, could help to reduce prejudice and improve relations among groups that are experiencing conflict. To be beneficial
in reducing prejudice and hostility it has been proposed that the contact situation must be characterised by positive intergroup relations, what Allport (1954,
p. 489) termed the 'optimal' conditions: equal status, intergroup cooperation,
common goals, and support by social and institutional authorities. An extensive critique of contact theory can be found in Vezzali and Stathi (2017) with an
in-depth review of this work provided by Lytle (2018).

Several writers have tried to clarify how contact in itself reduces prejudice
(Rothbart & John, 1985; Pettigrew, 1998; Hughes, Hewstone, Tausch, & Cairns,
2007; Everett, 2013). In particular, Pettigrew (1998, pp. 70–73) identified the
need for 'four processes of change': learning about the outgroup; changing behaviour; generating affective ties; and ingroup reappraisal. Likewise, according
to Everett (2013), contact effectively works through three mechanisms: cognitive (learning about the outgroup), behavioural (openness to positive contact
experiences), and affective (generating friendships).

For Hughes, Hewstone, Tausch, and Cairns (2007) it is when long-term
friendships are formed that the most influence is made in reducing prejudice.
As a result, it has been suggested that contact situations should be long enough
for different groups to get to know each other and to be comfortable with one
another. This is held as more important than cooperating together or learning
about the other group and is illustrated by the extended contact hypothesis,
that knowing that ingroup members have close relationships or friendships
with members of an outgroup can improve attitudes towards the outgroup
(Wright, Aron, McLaughlin-Volpe, & Ropp, 1997; and see Zhou, Page-Gould,
Aron, Moyer, & Hewstone, 2019 for a meta-analysis of twenty years of research
on the extended contact hypothesis).

In the first study from the Young People's Attitude to Religious Diversity
Project to operationalise the contact hypothesis, Francis, McKenna, and
Arweck (2019) focused specifically on countering anti-Muslim attitudes among
Christian and religiously unaffiliated students from England and Wales. To assess anti-Muslim attitudes they developed a seven-item scale and to assess
contact that focused specifically on friendship, employing the item 'I have
friends who are Muslims'.

In light of the accumulated findings from the Young People's Attitude to
Religious Diversity Project, the pressing research question (concerning the

connection between contact with Muslims and anti-Muslim attitude) needed to be contextualised within recognising the potentially contaminating effects of school factors (schools with a religious character or schools without a religious foundation), geographical factors (England, Wales, and London), personal factors (sex and age), psychological factors (employing the Eysenckian three-dimensional model of personality), and religious factors (differentiating among the three factors of self-assigned religious affiliation, religious belief, and religious practice).

The control variables identified above were selected for the following reasons. Differentiation between schools with a religious character and schools without a religious foundation has been noted on both theoretical and empirical grounds as potentially influencing attitudes toward religious diversity (see Francis & Village, 2014). Differentiation among the three geographical locations has been noted in light of the evidence of the 2011 census showing the different proportions of Muslims present in Wales, England, and London (see Office for National Statistics, 2012). Personal and social factors have been noted in light of the significant sex differences consistently found in religiosity (see Francis & Penny, 2014) and the significant changes that occur in religiosity during adolescence (see Kay & Francis, 1996). Psychological factors have been noted in light of the consistent findings that the Eysenckian three-dimensional model of personality (Eysenck & Eysenck, 1975, 1991) predict individual differences both in social attitudes (see Eysenck & Eysenck, 1975, 1976) and in religion-related attitudes (see Francis, 2009). Religious factors have been noted in light of the controversy regarding whether religious commitment promotes or frustrates acceptance of religious diversity (see Francis, Pyke, & Penny, 2015). Religious factors differentiate between self-assigned affiliation, public practice, and personal belief in light of the different effects of these diverse experiences of religiosity (see Francis & Village, 2014).

After taking these control variables into account, the data demonstrated the positive effect of having friends who are Muslim on lowering anti-Muslim attitudes. Given the potential significance of this finding for promoting good community relations within religiously diverse societies, McKenna and Francis (under review a) repeated the analyses in respect of the Sikh community developing a five-item scale to assess anti-Sikh attitudes, and McKenna and Francis (under review b) reported the analyses in respect of the Jewish community, developing a five-item scale to assess anti-Jewish attitudes. All three analyses demonstrated similar findings: having Muslim friends lowered anti-Muslim attitudes; having Sikh friends lowered anti-Sikh attitudes; and having Jewish friends lowered anti-Jewish attitude.

PSYCHOLOGICAL PERSPECTIVES ON RELIGIOUS EDUCATION   41

In many ways these findings may be the most important outcome for the Young People's Attitude to Religious Diversity Project in view of the pedagogical implications of these findings. For example, the key finding from the first study in the series indicated that young people who get to know Muslim peers as their friends are less likely to hold anti-Muslim attitudes. They are less likely to think that a lot of harm is done in the world by Muslims. They are less likely to feel that they would not like to live next door to Muslims. They are more likely to support the wearing of distinctive Muslim clothing in schools. They are more likely to be interested in finding out about Muslims. The problem is that not all young people have the opportunity to grow up alongside young Muslims and get to know them as friends.

Drawing on the findings from this research study Francis and ap Siôn (2019) discuss the journey from educational research into classroom practice. They argue that:

> The development of open and positive attitudes towards difference underpins respect for diversity. Foundations for open and positive attitudes need to be put in place during the early years. Open and positive attitudes grow from familiarity with and contact with diverse populations (the so-called contact hypothesis).

From these principles ap Siôn and Francis have developed, with sponsorship from the Welsh Government, two curriculum series, *Exploring Why* and *Exploring our World* for young learners (on open access at: http://www.st-marys-centre.org.uk).

These two series are designed to bring young learners into contact with young people from a variety of faith backgrounds. The central characters of these books are Aled and Siân. By identifying with them, young learners are brought into contact with Aled and Siân's friends. Aled and Siân themselves have no explicit religious identity. Yet through their friends they are welcomed not only into the world of young Muslims (Ahmed and Salma), but also into the world of young Christians (Peter and Mary) and young Jews (Nathan and Rachel).

Francis and ap Siôn (2019) argue that the natural curiosity displayed by Aled and Siân as they enter into the diverse worlds of their friends is infectious, and carries the young learner along with them on their journey of discovery. The consequence is that Aled and Siân gain access to deeper friendships and to richer experiences. The consequence is that the young learners who journey alongside Aled and Siân share vicariously in that experience. The consequence too is that Aled and Siân's friends who grow up within religious families may live happier and safer lives.

8 Psychological Type Theory for Ministry and Discipleship

The individual differences tradition in psychology has also stimulated research in and has implications for religious education and religious formation within the adult Christian community. Stimulated by an emerging 'theology of individual differences', as shaped by Francis and Village (2015b), a specific strand of personality theory has been shown to be fruitful in exploring discipleship learning and church ministry. This specific strand of personality theory known as 'psychological type' was inspired by Carl Jung (1971) and developed and operationalised by a series of psychometric instruments, including the Myers-Briggs Type Indicator (Myers & McCaulley, 1985), the Keirsey Temperament Sorter (Keirsey & Bates, 1978), and the Francis Psychological Type Scales (Francis, 2005b). The basic building blocks of psychological type theory distinguish between two orientations (extraversion and introversion), two perceiving functions (sensing and intuition), two judging functions (thinking and feeling), and two attitudes toward the outer world (judging and perceiving).

The two orientations are concerned with where energy is drawn from; energy can be gathered either from the outside world or from the inner world. Extraverts (E) are orientated toward the outside world; they are energised by the events and people around them. They enjoy communicating and thrive in stimulating and exciting environments. They prefer to act in a situation rather than reflect on it. They may vocalise a problem or an idea, rather than think it through privately. They may be drained by silence and solitude. They tend to focus their attention on what is happening outside themselves. They are usually open individuals, easy to get to know, and enjoy having many friends. In contrast, introverts (I) are orientated toward their inner world; they are energised by their inner ideas and concepts. They may feel drained by events and people around them. They prefer to reflect on a situation rather than act in it. They enjoy solitude, silence, and contemplation, as they tend to focus their attention on what is happening in their inner life. They may appear reserved and detached, and they may prefer to have a small circle of intimate friends rather than many acquaintances.

The perceiving functions are concerned with the way in which people receive and process information; this can be done through use of sensing or through use of intuition. Sensing types (S) tend to focus on specific details, rather than the overall picture. They are concerned with the actual, the real,

PSYCHOLOGICAL PERSPECTIVES ON RELIGIOUS EDUCATION 43

and the practical; and they tend to be down-to-earth and matter-of-fact. They may feel that particular details are more significant than general patterns. They are frequently fond of the traditional and conventional. They may be conservative and tend to prefer what is known and well-established. In contrast, intuitive types (N) focus on the possibilities of a situation, perceiving meanings, and relationships. They may feel that perception by the senses is not as valuable as information gained from the indirect associations that impact their perceptions. They focus on the overall picture, rather than specific facts and data. They follow their inspirations enthusiastically, but not always realistically. They can appear to be up in the air and may be seen as idealistic dreamers. They often aspire to bring innovative change to established conventions.

The judging functions are concerned with the way in which people make decisions and judgements; this can be done through use of objective impersonal logic or subjective interpersonal values. Thinking types (T) make judgements based on objective, impersonal logic. They value integrity and justice. They are known for their truthfulness and for their desire for fairness. They consider conforming to principles to be of more importance than cultivating harmony. They are often good at making difficult decisions as they are able to analyse problems in order to reach an unbiased and reasonable solution. They may consider it to be more important to be honest and correct than to be tactful, when working with others. In contrast, feeling types (F) make judgements based on subjective, personal values. They value compassion and mercy. They are known for their tactfulness and for their desire for peace. They are more concerned to promote harmony, than to adhere to abstract principles. They are able to take into account other people's feelings and values in decision-making and problem-solving, ensuring they reach a solution that satisfies everyone. They are often thought of as 'warm-hearted'. They may find it difficult to criticise others, even when it is necessary. They find it easy to empathise with other people and tend to be trusting and encouraging of others.

The attitudes toward the outside world are concerned with the way in which people respond to the world around them, either by imposing structure and order on that world or by remaining open and adaptable to the world around them. Judging types (J) have a planned, orderly approach to life. They enjoy routine and established patterns. They prefer to follow schedules in order to reach an established goal and may make use of lists, timetables, or diaries. They tend to be punctual, organised, and tidy. They may find it difficult to deal with unexpected disruptions of their plans. Likewise, they are inclined to be resistant to changes to established methods. They prefer to make decisions quickly and to stick to their conclusions once made. In contrast, perceiving types (P) have a flexible, open-ended approach to life. They enjoy change and spontaneity. They prefer to leave projects open in order to adapt and improve them. They may find plans and schedules restrictive and tend to be easygoing about issues such as punctuality, deadlines, and tidiness. Indeed, they may consider last minute pressure to be a necessary motivation in order to complete projects. They are often good at dealing with the unexpected. Indeed, they may welcome change and variety as routine bores them. Their behaviour may often seem impulsive and unplanned.

Psychological type data can be reported and interpreted in a number of different ways, drawing on the four dichotomous type preferences (the two orientations, the two perceiving functions, the two judging functions, and the two attitudes), on the 16 complete types (like ISTJ or ENFP), on the four dominant types (dominant sensing, dominant intuition, dominant feeling, or dominant thinking), or on the eight dominant and auxiliary pairs (like dominant thinking with auxiliary intuition or dominant intuition with auxiliary thinking).

Another perspective was provided by Keirsey and Bates (1978) who proposed an interpretive framework drawing on and distinguishing between four temperaments characterised as SJ, SP, NT, and NF. In the language shaped by Keirsey and Bates (1978) the Epimethean Temperament characterises the SJ profile, people who long to be dutiful and exist primarily to be useful to the social units to which they belong. The Dionysian Temperament characterises the SP profile, people who want to be engaged, involved, and doing something new. The Promethean Temperament characterises the NT profile, people who want to understand, explain, shape and predict realties, and who prize their personal competence. The Apollonian Temperament characterises the NF profile, people who quest for authenticity and for self-actualisation, who are idealistic, and who have great capacity for empathic listening.

The Francis Psychological Type Scales (Francis, 2005b) were designed specifically to operationalise type theory in a way suitable for including in large-scale surveys. The studies conducted among religious leaders and within church congregations have provided a good basis on which to test and to report on the internal consistency reliability of the Francis Psychological Type Scales across a range of different groups. Overall these four underlying scales (orientations, E and I; perceiving process, S and N; judging process, T and F; attitude, J and P) have generated alpha coefficients (Cronbach, 1951) well in excess of the threshold of .65 recommended by DeVellis (2003). For example, in Australia among 212 clergywomen from 14 denominations, Robbins, Francis, and Powell (2012) reported alpha coefficients of .84 for the EI Scale, .79 for the SN Scale, .71 for the TF Scale, and .81 for the JP Scale. In England among 1,047 Anglican clergy, Village (2011) reported alpha coefficients of .85 for the

PSYCHOLOGICAL PERSPECTIVES ON RELIGIOUS EDUCATION

EI Scale, .77 for the SN Scale, .72 for the TF Scale, and .81 for the JP Scale. In the USA among 748 clergy serving within the Presbyterian Church (USA), Francis, Wulff, and Robbins (2008) reported alpha coefficients of .85 for the EI Scale, .76 for the SN Scale, .72 for the TF Scale, and .79 for the JP Scale.

Two other studies by Francis, Laycock, and Brewster (2017) on data from 722 Anglican clergy in England, and by Payne, Lewis, and Francis (under review) have reported on the factor structure of the Francis Psychological Type Scale. For example, Payne, Lewis, and Francis (under review) reported that the varimax rotated solution with Kaiser normalisation recovered the hypothesised location of 39 of the 40 pairs of items across four factors with factor weightings above .38.

As well as reporting on the psychological type profile of church leaders and religious professionals, the Francis Psychological Type Scales have been used to explore the variation among different religious communities. Studies that have employed the Francis Psychological Type Scales to map the profile of church congregations include surveys conducted among 3,304 participants attending 140 Anglican congregations in England (Francis, Robbins, & Craig, 2011), 1,527 churchgoers from a range of different Christian denominations in Australia (Robbins & Francis, 2011), 1,474 churchgoing Roman Catholics in Australia (Robbins & Francis, 2012), 1,156 churchgoers from a range of Christian denominations in England (Village, Baker, & Howat, 2012), and 105 Greek Orthodox churchgoers in London (Lewis, Varvatsoulias, & Williams, 2012). Building on such studies of regular congregations, three recent studies have reported on the psychological type profile of participants engaged in various forms of Fresh Expressions of Church (Francis, Clymo, & Robbins, 2014; Village, 2015; Francis, Wright, & Robbins, 2016). A second set of studies has reported on the psychological type profile of participants engaged in cathedral congregations (Lankshear & Francis, 2015; Walker, 2012). A third set of studies has looked at churchgoers alongside Muslims (Francis & Datoo, 2012), online atheists (Baker & Robbins, 2012), and those engaged in the 'Church of Implicit Religion' (Francis & ap Siôn, 2013).

Working with colleagues on in-service development programmes for clergy, Francis noted that the ways in which clergy seemed to reflect their preferred psychological type characteristics in the way in which they interpreted and experienced parish ministry. In order to test this theory, Payne and Francis (2002) developed and tested the Payne Index of Ministry Styles (PIMS). This index proposed eight seven-item scales that attempted to capture the distinctive emphases in ministry consistent with the eight constructs of psychological type theory: introversion and extraversion, sensing and intuition, thinking and feeling, and judging and perceiving. For example, introverts may be more vitalised by praying for people, while extraverts may be more vitalised by visiting people.

Drawing on data provided by 191 Church in Wales clergy who completed both the Payne Index of Ministry Styles and the Myers-Briggs Type Indicator (Myers & McCaulley, 1985), Francis and Payne (2002) demonstrated the psychometric properties of their new measure, and charted the complex ways in which personal psychological type preferences influence ministry styles. For example, while extraverts were able to avoid engagement with aspects of introverted ministry styles, introverts were less able to avoid engagement with aspects of extraverted ministry styles. This finding alerts introverted ministers to develop strategies that may protect them from the energy depletion that arises from working outside their preferred model of engagement.

In order to explore the connection between psychological type and ministry styles, Smith and Francis designed a series of qualitative studies in which both experienced and newly ordained clergy explored their experiences of ministry and their preferred ministry styles in small groups designed to bring those of like type preferences together (see Smith, 2015a, 2015b, 2018; Francis & Smith, 2015, 2016; Smith & Francis, 2015). These data too demonstrated the relevance of the individual differences approach to appreciating diversity in approaches to ministry.

Working with colleagues on a BA in theology for discipleship and ministry, Francis (2015a) noted the ways in which individuals' ways of learning seemed to reflect their preferred psychological type characteristics. In order to test this theory, Francis and Robbins (2015) developed the Francis Index of Learning Styles (FILS). This index proposed eight ten-item scales that attempted to capture the distinctive emphases in learning consistent with the eight constructs of psychological type theory. For example, introverts may find that thinking alone about the course materials helped them to clarify what they thought, while extraverts may find that talking with others helped them to clarify what they thought.

Drawing on data provided by 108 course participants who completed both the Francis Index of Learning Styles and the Francis Psychological Type Scales (Francis, 2005), Francis and Robbins (2015) found that the learning community comprised more introverts (66%) than extraverts (34%), more sensing types (67%) than intuitive types (33%), more judging types (79%) than perceiving types (21%), and a balance between thinking types (49%) and feeling types (51%). The data also demonstrated that the group as a whole appreciated the way in which the programme intentionally blended teaching and learning styles designed to be inclusive of individual differences in learning preferences.

9 Biblical Hermeneutics and Homiletics

Working with colleagues engaged in teaching biblical hermeneutics and homiletics, Francis noted the ways in which individuals interpreted scripture and proclaimed scripture seemed to reflect their preferred perceiving function (sensing or intuition) and their preferred judging function (thinking or feeling). Locating this insight within the wider framework of the reader approach to biblical hermeneutics, it seemed reasonable to hypothesise that scriptural interpretation was as likely to be influenced by the psychological context of the reader as by the sociological context prioritised by the reader perspective approach (see Segovia & Tolbert, 1995a, 1995b).

Psychological perspectives in biblical interpretation embrace two different approaches rooted within psychological theories and psychological methods. The first approach places the weight on the text itself. It is this approach that characterises contributions to the Psychology and Bible programme unit of the Society of Biblical Literature (see Ellens, 2012) and is exemplified through the following family of studies by Rollins (1999), Kille (2001), Ellen and Rollins (2004), and Rollins and Kille (2007). In this approach, psychological constructs are used as the lenses through which particular biblical texts, themes, or characters are viewed and interpreted, in ways similar to those employed by scholars using feminist, liberationist, or ethnic lenses.

The second approach places the weight on the reader and is related both to wider reader-response theory (Bleich, 1978; Fish, 1980; Booth, 1984) and to the reader-perspective approach to biblical hermeneutics as originally shaped by attention on the social location of the reader in terms of factors such as gender and ethnicity. The idea that the reader perspective might be shaped by the psychological type profile of the reader, drawing on psychological type theory as proposed by Jung (1971), was advanced in a couple of early papers by Stiefel (1992) and Bassett, Mathewson, and Gailitis (1993) and subsequently developed into the SIFT (Sensing, Intuition, Feeling, Thinking) approach to biblical hermeneutics and liturgical preaching in a series of theoretically driven studies by Francis and Atkins (2000, 2001, 2002). Building on these foundations, Francis and Village (2008) extrapolated from psychological type theory to characterise the kind of reading and proclamation that would be associated with the two perceiving functions (sensing and intuition) and with the two judging functions (thinking and feeling).

Francis and Village (2008) argued that for sensing types, interpreting a text may be largely about attending to what is actually there. They will value interpretations that highlight the details in the text, especially those that draw on sensory information. Interpretations that begin with a repeat of the text and draw attention to details will appeal to sensing types, who will be reluctant to speculate too widely about hidden or metaphorical meanings. The sensing function draws attention to factual details, so sensing types will be likely to interpret biblical passages literally rather than symbolically or metaphorically.

For intuitive types, interpreting a text may be largely about using the text as a springboard to imaginative ideas. They will be inspired by interpretations that fire the imagination and raise new possibilities and challenges. Interpretations that raise wider questions and that look for overarching or underlying concepts will appeal to intuitive types, who may find the plain or literal sense rather uninteresting. Intuitive types find it natural to make links between analogous ideas and concepts, and they will be likely to interpret passages symbolically or metaphorically, rather than literally.

For feeling types, interpreting a text may be largely about applying the human dimensions to present day issues of compassion, harmony, and trust. They will be drawn to empathizing with the characters in a narrative, and will want to understand their thoughts, motives, and emotions. Interpretations that try to understand what it was like to be there will appeal to feeling types, who may be less interested in the abstract theological ideas that might be drawn from the text.

For thinking types interpreting a text may largely be about seeing what the text means in terms of evidence, moral principles, or theology. They will be drawn to using rationality and logic to identify the ideas and truth-claims in a text. Interpretations that highlight the theological claims in a text will appeal to thinking types, who may be less interested in trying to understand the characters described by the text.

In order to test this theory, workshops have been arranged in a variety of locations to enable participants to experience their interpretation of scripture in type-alike groups. For example, participants may be organised into groups according to their perceiving preferences, distinguishing among high scoring sensing types, high scoring intuitive types, and less well-defined perceiving preferences; or according to their judging preferences, distinguishing among high scoring feeling types, high scoring thinking types, and less well-defined judging preferences. The experience of working in type-alike groups facilitates like-minded participants to develop their distinctive type-related voice. Sensing types are good at examining the detailed text. Intuitive types are good at spotting the big themes and making the connections. Feeling types are good at responding to the values and to the people. Thinking types are good at identifying the theological issues at stake and exploring the difficulties raised in the text. From these workshops it also becomes evident how psychological type profile influences the message proclaimed from the pulpit.

PSYCHOLOGICAL PERSPECTIVES ON RELIGIOUS EDUCATION

These type-alike workshops originally focused on passages from the four Gospels including: the feeding of the five thousand reported in Mark 6:34–44 (Francis, 2010); the resurrection narratives reported in Mark 16:1–8 and Matthew 28:1–15 (Francis & Jones, 2011); the cleansing of the Temple and the incident of the fig tree reported in Mark 11:11–21 (Francis, 2012a; Francis & ap Siôn, 2016b); the Johannine feeding narrative reported in John 6:4–22 (Francis, 2012b); the narrative of separating sheep from goats reported in Matthew 25:31–46 (Francis & Smith, 2012); the birth narratives reported in Matthew 2:13–20 and Luke 2:8–16 (Francis & Smith, 2013); two narratives concerning John the Baptist reported in Mark 1:2–8 and Luke 3:2b–20 (Francis, 2013; Francis & Smith, 2014); the Johannine feeding narrative reported in John 6:5–15 (Francis & Jones, 2014); two passages from Mark exploring different aspects of discipleship reported in Mark 6:7–14 and Mark 6:33–41 (Francis & Jones, 2015a); the foot washing account reported in John 13:2b–15 (Francis, 2015b); two healing narratives reported in Mark 2:1–12 and Mark 10:46–52 (Francis & Jones, 2015b); the narrative of blind Bartimaeus reported in Mark 10:46–52 (Smith & Francis, 2016); the Road to Emmaus narrative reported in Luke 24:13–35 (Francis & ap Siôn, 2016a; Francis & Smith, 2017); the Lucan call of the first disciples reported in Luke 5:1–7 (Francis & ap Siôn, 2017); the missionary journey reported in Mark 6:6b–16 (Francis, Smith, & Francis-Dehqani, 2017); the material on Pilate and Judas reported in Matthew 27:3–10, 19–25 (Francis & Ross, 2018); the teaching of Jesus concerning the birds and the lilies, and concerning the labourers in the vineyard in Matthew 6:25–30 and 20:1–15 (Francis, Smith, & Francis-Dehqani, 2018); the account of the lost sheep in Matthew 18:10–14 (Jones & Francis, 2019); the strategy for church disciplinary procedures proposed in Matthew 18:15–18 (Francis, Jones, & Hebden, 2019); and the account of the baptism of Jesus in Mark 1:4–15 (Francis, Jones, & Martinson, 2019). Likewise, this approach has also been applied to Psalms (Francis & Smith, 2018; Francis, Smith, & Corio, 2018; Francis, McKenna, & Sahin, 2018). This research tradition has also been developed in Poland by Chaim (2013, 2014, 2015).

A good illustration of the way in which the SIFT preaching workshops operate is provided by the study on the Matthean pericopes on Pilate and Judas conducted among 24 experienced preachers by Francis and Ross (2018). These passages are of particular interest to biblical scholars because they have been added by Matthew to Mark's text in order to amplify his understanding of the problematic behaviour of Pilate and Judas. The two pericopes added within Matthew 27:19–25 (concerning Pilate) are both rich in material to engage the perceiving functions (sensing and intuition). The pericope added within Matthew 27:3–10 (concerning Judas) is rich in material to engage the judging functions (thinking and feeling). The opportunity to structure workshops to explore these two passages of scripture within type-alike groups of experienced preachers was provided by a full-day programme convened by Waterloo Lutheran Seminary during the week before Holy Week 2017 as part of the seminary's commitment to the continuing professional development of clergy. The week before Holy Week was an ideal time for helping clergy to focus on the Passion Narrative.

Following an introduction to the theology of individual differences and to psychological type theory, participants were invited to complete a recognised measure of psychological type and to select their best fit on the four preferences between introversion and extraversion, between sensing and intuition, between thinking and feeling, and between judging and perceiving. They were then invited to participate in two hermeneutical communities. The first hermeneutical community was structured on the basis of the perceiving process, and explored Matthew 27:19–25 through the lenses of sensing and intuition. The second hermeneutical community was structured on the basis of the judging process and explored Matthew 27:3–10 through the lenses of thinking and feeling. Each of these hermeneutical communities was divided into four groups: in the first case, one group of high scoring sensing types, one group of high scoring intuitive types, and two groups of lower scoring types; in the second case, one group of high scoring thinking types, one group of high scoring feeling types, and two groups of lower scoring types. Each group was asked to nominate one of the members to document and to feed back to the plenary session.

Two main observations arise from working in this way. The first observation arises in the groups themselves. When sensing types are working together in a group, and are not disturbed by intuitive types, they focus clearly on examining the detailed material in front of them. When intuitive types are working together in a group, and are not disturbed by sensing types, they quickly abandon the detailed material in front of them and a wide range of imaginative ideas emerge. When feeling types are working together in a group, and are not disturbed by thinking types, they become observed in the human narrative and fight shy of the tough issues. When thinking types are working together in a group, and are not disturbed by feeling types, their powers of analysis flourish and they lose sight of the human consequences of their strategy.

The second observation emerges when the groups report back to the plenary session. Sensing types are annoyed and confused by the wide range of ideas generated by intuitive types. Intuitive types are annoyed and easily bored by the level of details examined by sensing types. Feeling types are amazed and

PSYCHOLOGICAL PERSPECTIVES ON RELIGIOUS EDUCATION

sometimes hurt by the toughminded analysis of thinking types. Thinking types are amazed by and sometimes despair at the way feeling types try to avoid conflict and settle for compromise.

10   Religious Orientation Theory and Motivational Styles

Several strands within the individual differences tradition offer insights into ways in which adult churchgoers may differ in their approach to religion. Religious orientation theory, concerned with primary motivation for religious engagement, has been one of the most influential developments in this field, resulting in a substantial literature of empirical research.

Within the existing large body of empirical research, the measures of religious orientation have been used both appropriately and inappropriately. In distinguishing between these two uses the conceptual problem concerns clarifying where the notion of religious orientation fits alongside other aspects or dimensions of religion as operationalised within the social sciences. In its origin the notion of measuring religious orientation is very different from the notions of measuring, say, religious affiliation, religious practice, or attitude toward religion. Questions regarding religious affiliation are generally designed to categorise individuals according to whether or not they align themselves with a religious group. Questions regarding religious practice are generally designed to grade individuals according to the frequency with which they engage with personal or public religious behaviours. Questions regarding attitude toward religion are generally designed to locate individuals along a continuum ranging from a negative to a positive view of religion. In other words, all three notions of self-assigned religious affiliation, religious practice, and attitude toward religion are designed to distinguish, in one way or another, between individuals high in religiosity and individuals low in religiosity. The notion of religious orientation, however, provides a very different construct. The measurement of religious orientation is intended first and foremost to distinguish different ways of being religious among those who, by some other criteria, can be described as religious.

The two terms intrinsic religiosity and extrinsic religiosity were given clear currency by the pioneering work of Gordon Allport. According to Allport (1966, p. 454), this distinction separated churchgoers whose communal type of membership supports and serves other, non-religious ends, from those for whom religion is an end in itself—a final, not instrumental, good. Allport proceeded to argue as follows about the nature of extrinsic orientation.

> While there are several varieties of extrinsic religious orientation, we may say they all point to a type of religion that is strictly utilitarian: useful for the self in granting safety, social standing, solace, and endorsement for one's chosen way of life.
>
> ALLPORT, 1966, p. 455

Regarding the nature of intrinsic orientation, Allport made the following case.

> The intrinsic form of the religious sentiment regards faith as a supreme value in its own right.... A religious sentiment of this sort floods the whole life with motivations and meaning. Religion is no longer limited to single segments of self-interest.
>
> ALLPORT, 1966, p. 455

In a subsequent (and now classic) co-authored paper, Allport and Ross (1967) developed the understanding of the distinction between intrinsic and extrinsic orientation in the following way. Here is their description of the extrinsic orientation.

> Persons with this orientation are disposed to use religion for their own ends. The term is borrowed from axiology, to designate an interest that is held because it serves other, more ultimate interests. Extrinsic values are always instrumental and utilitarian. Persons with this orientation may find religion useful in a variety of ways—to provide security and solace, sociability and distraction, status and self-justification. The embraced creed is lightly held or else selectively shaped to fit more primary needs. In theological terms the extrinsic type turns to God, but without turning away from self.
>
> ALLPORT & ROSS, 1967, p. 434

Here is their description of the intrinsic orientation.

> Persons with this orientation find their master motive in religion. Other needs, strong as they may be, are regarded as of less ultimate significance, and they are, so far as possible, brought into harmony with the religious beliefs and prescriptions. Having embraced a creed the individual endeavours to internalize it and follow it fully. It is in this sense that he lives his religion.
>
> ALLPORT & ROSS, 1967, p. 434

PSYCHOLOGICAL PERSPECTIVES ON RELIGIOUS EDUCATION 53

Allport and Ross (1967) proposed two scales to measure their dimensions of intrinsic and extrinsic orientation. The intrinsic measure contained nine items, the first two of which were: 'It is important for me to spend periods of time in private religious thought and meditation'; 'If not prevented by unavoidable circumstances, I attend church'. The extrinsic measure contained eleven items, the first two of which were: 'Although I believe in my religion, I feel there are many more important things in my life'; 'It doesn't matter so much what I believe so long as I lead a moral life'.

The measures of intrinsic and extrinsic orientation developed by Allport and Ross (1967) demonstrated that individuals could occupy four locations defined on these two dimensions. Those who recorded high scores on the intrinsic scale and low scores on the extrinsic scale were defined as 'pure intrinsic' orientation. Those who recorded high scores on the extrinsic scale and low scores on the intrinsic scale were defined as 'pure extrinsic' orientation. Those who recorded high scores on the extrinsic scale and high scores on the intrinsic scale were defined as 'indiscriminantly pro-religious'. Those who recorded low scores on the extrinsic scale and low scores on the intrinsic scale were defined as 'indiscriminantly anti-religious' (Hood, 1978).

Critiquing Allport's model of religious orientation, Batson (1976) and Batson and Ventis (1982) argued the case for a third dimension alongside the intrinsic and extrinsic orientations, which they styled the quest orientation. The quest orientation gave recognition to a form of religiosity which embraces characteristics of complexity, doubt, tentativeness, and honesty in facing existential questions. Batson and Ventis provided the following description of the quest orientation.

> An individual who approaches religion in this way recognises that he or she does not know, and probably never will know, the final truth about such matters. But still the questions are deemed important, and however tentative and subject to change, answers are sought. There may not be a clear belief in a transcendent reality, but there is a transcendent, religious dimension to the individual's life.
>
> BATSON & VENTIS, 1982, p. 150

Batson and Ventis (1982, p. 145) also provided a six-item instrument to measure the quest orientation. Two items were: 'It might be said that I value my religious doubts and uncertainties'; 'Questions are far more central to my religious experience than are answers'. Subsequently Batson and Schoenrade (1991a, 1991b) developed a longer twelve-item quest scale, which dropped one item from the original six-item scale (My religious development has emerged out of my growing sense of personal identity) and introduced seven new items.

Batson, Schoenrade and Ventis (1993, p. 174) emphasised two key characteristics of their understanding of the three-dimensional model of being religious (intrinsic, extrinsic, and quest). First, they argued against using the scales to assign individuals to types. They wrote as follows.

> We have not classified religious individuals as being of a means type, end type, or quest type. Instead, we have measured the degree to which each individual's religion can be characterised in each of these ways. Each individual receives a score on each component, and each component is a continuous dimension.
>
> BATSON, SCHOENRADE, & VENTIS, 1993, p. 174

Second, they maintained that the three dimensions in their model are independent of one another, as established by orthogonal factor analysis. They wrote as follows.

> How you score on one component says precisely nothing about how you will score on the other two. The three are independent dimensions. You might score high on all three components, low on all three (if you are relatively nonreligious), or high on one or two and low on another.
>
> BATSON, SCHOENRADE, & VENTIS, 1993, p. 174

Francis (2007) undertook a thorough review of existing research within the field of religious orientation. In the light of this review Francis proposed the New Indices of Religious Orientation and made the clear recommendation that these scales were not intended to distinguish between religious and irreligious individuals, but to distinguish between different motivations among those who are religious.

The New Indices of Religious Orientation were designed to propose scales of equal length to measure each of the three constructs (intrinsic orientation, extrinsic orientation, and quest orientation), and to give equal weight to the three conceptual components identified within each construct. Batson and Schoenrade (1991b) defined the three components of quest orientation as: readiness to face existential questions without reducing their complexity; self-criticism and perception of religious doubt as positive; openness to change. The three conceptual components of extrinsic orientation are: compartmentalisation, or the separation of religion from the rest of life; social support, or the use of religion to achieve social ends; personal support, or the use of

PSYCHOLOGICAL PERSPECTIVES ON RELIGIOUS EDUCATION

religion to gain personal comfort. The three conceptual components of intrinsic orientation are: integration, or the close relationship between religion and the rest of life; public religion, or the importance given to church for religious ends; personal religion, or the importance given to personal prayer and reading for religious ends. Within the New Indices of Religious Orientation each of the nine conceptual components is represented by three items, thus comprising three nine-item scales. Data provided by 517 undergraduate students in Wales demonstrated the satisfactory psychometric properties of these instruments (Francis, 2007).

Working within the individual differences tradition the connection between psychological type and religious motivation has been explored by three empirical studies. In an initial exploratory study, Francis and Ross (2000) suggested that a key focus of theoretical interest concerned the connection between the perceiving process and the quest orientation. Drawing on the discussion advanced by Ross (1992), they argued that intuitive types are intrigued by complexity and are likely to endorse the view that doubt strengthens faith (thus recording higher scores on the quest scale). Their study, however, employing data provided by a sample of 64 active adult Catholic churchgoers who completed the Myers Briggs Type Indicator (Myers & McCaulley, 1985) together with the six-item measure of the quest orientation proposed by Batson and Ventis (1982), failed to support this hypothesis. This study may have been flawed not only by the small sample but, more importantly, by the homogeneity of the participants.

In a second study, Ross and Francis (2010) employed data provided by a diverse sample of 481 weekly churchgoing Christians who completed the Myers-Briggs Type Indicator (Myers & McCaulley, 1985) together with the nine-item measure of the quest orientation proposed by Francis (2007) in the NIRO. The diverse sample of weekly churchgoers comprised Anglicans (68%), Pentecostals (20%), Baptists (5%), Methodists (3%), Catholics (3%), and Presbyterians (1%). This study recorded a significantly higher mean score on the quest orientation among intuitive types than among sensing types.

In a third study, Walker (2015) employed data provided by 390 individuals attending a Christmas carol service in an Anglican cathedral who completed the Francis Psychological Type Scales (Francis, 2005) together with the nine-item measure of the quest orientation proposed by Francis (2007) in the NIRO. These participants evidenced a wide range of frequency of church attendance, with 20% attending weekly or more, 12% nearly weekly, 9% at least monthly, 14% at least six times per year, and 37% at least once a year. A further 9% claimed never to attend church suggesting that they did not regard attending a cathedral carol service as equating with church attendance. This study also recorded a significantly higher mean score on the quest orientation among intuitive types than among sensing types. In this study, Walker (2015) took the analysis one step further than the previous two articles by introducing temperament theory. A significantly lower mean score on the quest orientation was recorded by the SJ Epimethean Temperament than by the other three temperaments combined.

In a subsequent study, Francis and Lankshear (under review) set out to explore the potential distinctiveness of congregations at Southwark Cathedral, a cathedral in south London that has a long tradition of proclaiming an inclusive and liberal gospel. The potential distinctiveness of congregations at the cathedral was assessed through two distinctive theoretical frameworks, one rooted in psychological type theory and temperament theory, and the other rooted in religious orientation theory and religious motivation.

In terms of psychological type theory and temperament theory, it was hypothesised that individuals attracted to this kind of cathedral congregation would differ from the profile of Anglican church congregations published by Francis, Robbins, and Craig (2011), and re-presented by Francis, Wright, and Robbins (2016) in two main ways: that there would be a higher proportion of intuitive types in the cathedral congregation; and that there would be a lower proportion of the SJ Epimethean Temperament in the cathedral congregation. Both hypotheses were supported by the data.

In terms of religious orientation theory, it was hypothesised that the type of individuals attracted to the cathedral congregation would record higher scores on the measure of quest religious orientation for two reasons: that intuitive types would be more open to quest religiosity than sensing types; and that the SJ Epimethean Temperament would be less open to quest religiosity than the other temperaments. Both hypotheses were supported by the data.

Reflecting on these findings, Francis and Lankshear (under review) concluded that appreciation of the distinctive psychological type and temperament profile of different churches and different congregations (coupled with appreciation of the connection between this psychological profile and religious orientation and motivation) may be important and helpful for those with responsibility for leading churches and congregations. Clearly not all churches and congregations are alike. While in many churches, dominated by the SJ Epimethean Temperament, the preacher may not be applauded for asking unsettling questions or for challenging long-held doctrines and beliefs, in places like Southwark Cathedral such a preacher is likely to be applauded. Far from undermining the style of faith valued by many people in the congregation, such unsettling questions may well feed their faith, deepen their commitment to that religious quest, and confirm them in the conviction that their preacher, church, and congregation provide an appropriate and accepting context in which their style of faith can continue to be valued and nurtured.

Conclusion

This publication has set out to illustrate and to explore the contribution of the individual differences tradition within psychology to the field of religious education. In this exploration religious education was construed broadly to include the activity of schools, churches, and households, and to include children, young people, and adults. The contribution of the individual differences tradition has been illustrated by reference to nine main themes that have characterised consistent research in the field over the past four decades. These themes have included: the focus on religious affect as the dimension of religion that may get closest to the heart of the matter; the range of correlates that emerge in relation to individual differences in religious affect; the connection between personality and individual differences in religious affect; the explanations for sex differences in religion; the impact of church schools and households on religious formation; the identification and measurement of individual differences in religious motivation theory and religious orientation theory; the factors associated with individual differences in attitude toward religious diversity; the relevance of psychological type theory for ministry and discipleship; and the relevance of psychological type theory for biblical hermeneutics and homiletics.

The pattern that has emerged across these nine themes has been the consistent interplay between the conceptualisation of the research problem, the operationalisation of the research problem through clear measurement and data analysis, and the persistent replication of studies in order to distinguish between recurrent findings and less secure conclusions. Throughout the sections that have discussed these themes, it has become clear that more research is needed to test, to replicate, and to extend what has so far been achieved. In drawing together material for this publication, my aim has been to encourage a new generation of scholars to build on the foundations that are already secure, and also to take the project of an individual differences approach to the field of religious education in new directions, responding appropriately as new research questions emerge.

References

Abu-Ali, A., & Reisen, C. A. (1999). Gender role identity among adolescent Muslim girls living in the US. *Current Psychology: A journal for diverse perspectives on diverse psychological issues, 18*, 185–192.

Adamson, G., Shevlin, M., Lloyd, N. S. V., & Lewis, C. A. (2000). An integrated approach for assessing reliability and validity: An application of structural equation modelling to the measurement of religiosity. *Personality and Individual Differences, 29*, 971–979.

Aghababaei, N. (2016). Scientific faith and positive psychological functioning. *Mental Health, Religion and Culture, 7*, 734–741.

Akinyele, S., & Akinyele, T. (2007). Gender differences and church member satisfaction: An appraisal. *Gender & Behaviour, 5*, 1433–1442.

Alatopoulos, C. S. (1968). *A study of relationship between religious knowledge and certain social and moral attitudes among school leavers.* Unpublished M.Phil. dissertation, University of London.

Allport, G. W. (1954). *The nature of prejudice.* Cambridge, MA: Perseus Books.

Allport, G. W. (1966). Religious context of prejudice. *Journal for the Scientific Study of Religion, 5*, 447–457.

Allport, G. W., & Ross, J. M. (1967). Personal religious orientation and prejudice. *Journal of Personality and Social Psychology, 5*, 432–443.

Anthony, F. V., Hermans, C. A. M., & Sherkat, C. (2010). A comparative study of mystical experience among Christian, Muslim, and Hindu Students in Tamil Nadu, India. *Journal for the Scientific Study of Religion, 49*, 264–277.

ap Siôn, T. (2017). Seeing how we see each other: Learning from quantitative research among young people in the UK. *Journal of Beliefs and Values, 38*, 305–317.

Argyle, M. (1958). *Religious behaviour.* London: Routledge and Kegan Paul.

Argyle, M., & Beit-Hallahmi, B. (1975). *The social psychology of religion.* London: Routledge and Kegan Paul.

Argyle, M., Martin, M., & Crossland, J. (1989). Happiness as a function of personality and social encounters. In J. P. Forgas & J. M. Innes (Eds.), *Recent advances in social psychology: An international perspective* (pp. 189–203). Amsterdam, North Holland: Elsevier Science Publishers.

Arweck, E. (2017). *Young people's attitudes to religious diversity.* Abingdon: Routledge.

Astley, J., & Francis, L. J. (2010). Promoting positive attitudes toward science and religion among sixth-form pupils: Dealing with scientism and creationism. *British Journal of Religious Education, 32*, 189–200.

Astley, J., & Francis, L. J. (2016). Introducing the Astley-Francis Theology of Religions Index (AFTRI): Construct validity among 13- to 15-year-old students. *Journal of Beliefs and Values, 37*, 29–39.

Astley, J., Francis, L. J., & Robbins, M. (2012). Assessing attitude toward religion: The Astley-Francis Scale of Attitude toward Theistic Faith, *British Journal of Religious Education, 34*, 183–193.

Attfield, D. (1974). A fresh look at Goldman: The research needed today. *Learning for Living, 14*, 44–49.

Bailey, E. I. (1997). *Implicit religion in contemporary society.* Kampen, Netherlands: Kok Pharos.

Bailey, E. I. (1998). *Implicit religion: An introduction.* London: Middlesex University Press.

Bailey, E. I. (Ed.) (2002). *The secular quest for meaning in life: Denton papers in implicit religion.* New York: The Edwin Mellon Press Ltd.

Baker, J. O. (2008). An investigation of the sociological patterns of prayer frequency and content. *Sociology Review, 69*, 169–185.

Baker, M. J., & Robbins, M. (2012). American online atheists and psychological type. *Mental Health, Religion and Culture, 15*(10), 1077–1084.

Bartkowski, J. P., & Hempel, L. M. (2009). Sex and gender traditionalism among conservative Protestants: Does the difference make a difference? *Journal for the Scientific Study of Religion, 48*, 805–816.

Bassett, R. L., Mathewson, K., & Gailitis, A. (1993). Recognising the person in biblical interpretation: An empirical study. *Journal of Psychology and Christianity, 12*, 38–46.

Batson, C. D. (1976). Religion as prosocial: Agent or double agent? *Journal for the Scientific Study of Religion, 15*, 29–45.

Batson, C. D., & Schoenrade, P. A. (1991a). Measuring religion as quest: Reliability concerns. *Journal for the Scientific Study of Religion, 30*, 430–447.

Batson, C. D., & Schoenrade, P. A. (1991b). Measuring religion as quest: Validity concerns. *Journal for the Scientific Study of Religion, 30*, 416–429.

Batson, C. D., Schoenrade, P., & Ventis, W. L. (1993). *Religion and the individual: A social-psychological perspective.* Oxford: Oxford University Press.

Batson, C. D., & Ventis, W. L. (1982). *The religious experience: A social psychological perspective.* New York: Oxford University Press.

Beit-Hallahmi, B., & Argyle, M. (1997). *The psychology of religious behaviour, belief and experience.* London: Routledge.

Bellamy, J., Mou, S., & Castle, K., (2005). *Survey of church attenders aged 10- to 14-years: NCLS Occasional Paper.* Sydney, New South Wales: NCLS Research.

Bem, S. L. (1981). *Bem Sex Role Inventory: Professional manual.* Palo Alto, CA: Consulting Psychologists Press.

Bleich, D. (1978). *Subjective criticism.* Baltimore, MD: The Johns Hopkins University Press.

Booth, W. C. (1984). *The rhetoric of fiction.* Chicago, IL: University of Chicago Press.

Bourke, R., & Francis, L. J. (2000). Personality and religion among music students. *Pastoral Psychology*, *48*, 437–444.

Bourke, R., Francis, L. J., & Robbins, M. (2005). Personality and attitude toward Christianity among church musicians. *North American Journal of Psychology*, *7*, 85–88.

Bourke, R., Francis, L. J., & Robbins, M. (2007). Cattell's personality model and attitude toward Christianity. *Mental Health, Religion and Culture*, *10*, 353–362.

Brisco, H. (1969). A study of some aspects of the special contribution of Church of England aided primary schools to children's development, Unpublished M.Ed. dissertation, University of Liverpool.

Bull, N. J. (1969). *Moral judgement from childhood to adolescence*. London: Routledge and Kegan Paul.

Campo-Arias, A., & Ceballos-Ospino, G. A. (in press). Confirmatory factor analysis of the five-item version of the Francis Scale of Attitude toward Christianity in adolescent students. *Journal of Beliefs and Values*.

Campo-Arias, A., Herazo, E., & Oviedo, H. C. (2017). Estructura interna y confiabilidad de la escala breve de Francis en estudiantes de medicina [Internal structure and reliability of a five-item form of the Francis Scale in medical students]. *Pensamiento Psicológico*, *15*, 7–14.

Campo-Arias, A., Oviedo, H. C., & Cogollo, Z. (2009). Internal consistency of a five-item form of the Francis Scale of Attitude toward Christianity among adolescent students. *The Journal of Social Psychology*, *149*, 258–262.

Campo-Arias, A., Oviedo, H. C., Dtaz, C. F., & Cogollo, Z. (2006). Internal consistency of a Spanish translation of the Francis Scale of Attitude toward Christianity short form. *Psychological Reports*, *99*, 1008–1010.

Carter, M., Kay, W. K., & Francis, L. J. (1996). Personality and attitude toward Christianity among committed adult Christians. *Personality and Individual Differences*, *20*, 265–266.

Ceballos, G. A., Suescun, J. D., Oviedo, H. C., Herazo, E., & Campo-Arias, A. (2015). Five-item Francis Scale of Attitude toward Christianity: Construct and nomological validity and internal consistency among Colombian college students. *Journal of Beliefs and Values*, *36*, 347–353.

Chadwick, P. (1997). *Shifting alliances: Church and state in English education*. London: Cassell.

Chaim, W. (2013). Typy psychologiczne w recepcji i przekazie slowa bożego [Psychological typology in the reception and transmission of the Word of God]. *Roczniki Pastoralno-Katechetyczne*, *5*, 155–170.

Chaim, W. (2014). Metoda interpretacji i przepowiadania slowa bożego *SIFT* w służbie kaznodziejstwa cala dusza [The SIFT method in the service of preaching with all our souls]. *Roczniki Teologiczne*, *61*, 117–136.

Chaim, W. (2015). Profil typu psychologicznego, interpretacja biblii I głoszenie słowa bożego (badania empiryczne) [Psychological type profile, biblical hermeneutics and liturgical preaching (empirical research)]. *Resovia Sacra, 22*, 45–69.

Chamorro-Premuzic, T. (2007). *Personality and individual differences.* Oxford: Blackwell.

Church of England (2016). *Church of England vision for education: Deeply Christian, serving the common good.* London: Church of England Education Office.

Churches Information for Mission. (2001). *Faith in life: A snapshot of church life in England at the beginning of the twenty-first century.* London: Churches Information for Mission.

Cogollo, Z., Gómez-Bustamante, E. M., Herazo, E., & Campo-Arias, A. (2012). Validity and reliability of the five-item version of the Francis Scale of Attitude toward Christianity. *Revista de Facultad de Medicina, 60*, 103–110.

Costa, P. T., & McCrae, R. R. (1992). *Revised NEO Personality Inventory (NEO PI-R) and NEO Five Factor Inventory (NEO-FFI): Professional Manual.* Odessa, FL: Psychological Assessment Resources.

Cox, E. (1968). Honest to Goldman: An assessment. *Religious Education, 63*, 424–428.

Crea, G., Baioco, R., Ioverno, S., Buzzi, G., & Francis, L. J. (2014). The psychometric properties of the Italian translation of the Francis Scale of Attitude toward Christianity: A study among Catholic adolescents. *Journal of Beliefs and Values, 35*, 118–122.

Crockett, A., & Voas, D. (2006). Generations of decline: Religious change in 20th-century Britain. *Journal for the Scientific Study of Religion, 45*, 567–584.

Cronbach, L. J. (1951). Coefficient alpha and the internal structure of tests. *Psychometrika, 16*, 297–334.

Crozier, S., & Joseph, S. (1997). Religiosity and sphere-specific just world beliefs in 16- to 18-year olds. *Journal of Social Psychology, 137*, 510–513.

Cruickshank, M. (1963). *Church and state in English education.* London: Macmillan.

Darcy, F., & Beniskos, J. M. (1971). Some people say: The themes of resurrection and hell as perceived by 6- to 8-year-old children receiving religious instruction. *Lumen Vitae, 26*, 449–460.

Dent, H. J. (1947). *The Education Act 1944: Provisions, possibilities and some problems* (3rd ed.). London: University of London Press.

DeVellis, R. F. (2003). *Scale development: Theory and applications.* London: Sage.

Diduca, D., & Joseph, S. (1997). Schizotypal traits and dimensions of religiosity. *British Journal of Clinical Psychology, 36*, 635–638.

Dorahy, M. J., & Lewis, C. A. (2001). The relationship between dissociation and religiosity: An empirical evaluation of Schumaker's theory. *Journal for the Scientific Study of Religion, 40*, 317–324.

Dumoulin, A. (1971). The priest's occupations as perceived by 6–12 year old children. *Lumen Vitae, 26*, 316–332.

Durham Report (1970). *The Fourth R: The report of the commission on religious education in schools.* London: National Society and SPCK.

Eagle, D. (2011). Changing patterns of attendance at religious services in Canada, 1986–2008. *Journal for the Scientific Study of Religion, 50,* 187–200.

Eckert, R. M., & Lester, D. (1997). Altruism and religiosity. *Psychological Reports, 81,* 562.

Edwards, A. L. (1957). *Techniques of attitude scale construction.* New York: Appleton-Century-Crofts.

Eek, J. (2001). *Religious facilitation through intense liturgical participation: A quasi-experimental study of Swedish pilgrims to Taizé.* Lund: University of Lund Studies in Psychology of Religion.

Elken, A., Francis, L. J., & Robbins, M. (2010). The Estonian translation of the Francis Scale of Attitude toward Christianity: Internal consistency reliability and construct validity. *Journal of Beliefs and Values, 31,* 231–234.

Ellens, J. H. (2012). Psychology and biblical studies: Birth and development of a new SBL program unit (1991–2011). In J. H. Ellens (Ed.), *Psychological hermeneutics for biblical themes and texts: A festschrift in honour of Wayne G. Rollins* (pp. 21–42). London and New York: T & T Clark.

Ellens, J. H., & Rollins, W. G. (Eds.). (2004). *Psychology and the bible: A new way to read the scriptures* (Vol. 3: from Gospel to gnostics). Westport, CT: Praeger.

Esawi, A. R. M. (1968). *Ethico-religious attitudes and emotional adjustment in children aged 11–18 years.* Unpublished Ph.D. dissertation, University of Nottingham.

Evans, T. E., & Francis, L. J. (1996). Measuring attitude toward Christianity through the medium of Welsh. In L. J. Francis, W. K. Kay, & W. S. Campbell (Eds.), *Research in religious education* (pp. 279–294). Leominster: Fowler Wright Books.

Everett, J. A. C. (2013). Intergroup contact theory: past, present and future. *The Inquisitive Mind Magazine, 2* (17) http://www.in-mind.org/article/intergroup-contact -theory-past-present-and-future.

Eysenck, H. J. (1975). The structure of social attitudes. *British Journal of Social and Clinical Psychology, 14,* 323–331.

Eysenck, H. J. (1976). Structure of social attitudes. *Psychological Reports, 39,* 463–466.

Eysenck, H. J., Barrett, P., Wilson, G., & Jackson, C. (1992). Primary trait measurement of the 21 components of the PEN system. *European Journal of Psychological Assessment, 8,* 109–117.

Eysenck, H. J. & Eysenck, S. B. G. (1964). *Manual of the Eysenck Personality Inventory.* London: University of London Press.

Eysenck, H. J., & Eysenck, S. B. G. (1975). *Manual of the Eysenck Personality Questionnaire (adult and junior).* London: Hodder and Stoughton.

Eysenck, H. J., & Eysenck, S. B. G. (1976). *Psychoticism as a dimension of personality.* London: Hodder and Stoughton.

PSYCHOLOGICAL PERSPECTIVES ON RELIGIOUS EDUCATION 63

Eysenck, H. J., & Eysenck, S. B. G. (1991). *Manual of the Eysenck Personality Scales.* London: Hodder and Stoughton.

Eysenck, S. B. G., Easting, G., & Pearson, P. R. (1984). Age norms for impulsiveness in children. *Personality and Individual Differences, 5,* 315–321.

Eysenck, S. B. G., & Eysenck, H. J. (1963). On the dual nature of extraversion. *British Journal of Social and Clinical Psychology, 2,* 46–55.

Eysenck, S. B. G., Eysenck, H. J., & Barrett, P. (1985). A revised version of the psychoticism scale. *Personality and Individual Differences, 6,* 21–29.

Fagerlind, T. (1974). Research on religious education in the Swedish school system. *Character Potential, 7,* 38–47.

Farias, M., Newheiser, A.-K., Kahane, G., & de Toledo, Z. (2013). Scientific faith: Belief in science increases in the face of stress and existential anxiety. *Journal of Experimental Social Psychology, 49,* 1210–1213.

Fawcett, J., Andrews, V., & Lester, D. (2000). Religiosity and attitudes about abortion. *Psychological Reports, 87,* 980.

Fearn, M., Francis, L. J., & Wilcox, C. (2001). Attitude toward Christianity and psychological type: A survey among religious studies students. *Pastoral Psychology, 49,* 341–348.

Fearn, M., Lewis, C. A., & Francis, L. J. (2003). Religion and personality among religious studies students: A replication. *Psychological Reports, 93,* 819–822.

Ferreira, V., & Neto, F. (2002). Psychometric properties of the Francis Scale of Attitude toward Christianity among Portugese university students. *Psychological Reports, 91,* 995–998.

Fish, S. (1980). *Is there a text in this class?* Cambridge, MA: Harvard University Press.

Flavell, J. H. (1963). *The developmental psychology of Jean Piaget.* New York: Van Nostrand Reinhold Company.

Flere, S., Francis, L. J., & Robbins, M. (2011). The psychometric properties of the Serbian translation of the Francis Scale of Attitude toward Christianity: A study among Eastern Orthodox students. *Pastoral Psychology, 60,* 217–222.

Flere, S., Klanjsek, R., Francis, L. J., & Robbins, M. (2008). The psychometric properties of the Slovenian translation of the Francis Scale of Attitude toward Christianity: A study among Roman Catholic undergraduate students. *Journal of Beliefs and Values, 29,* 313–319.

Francis, L. J. (1976). *An enquiry into the concept 'readiness for religion'.* Unpublished Ph.D. dissertation. University of Cambridge.

Francis, L. J. (1978a). Attitude and longitude: A study in measurement. *Character Potential, 8,* 119–130.

Francis, L. J. (1978b). Measurement reapplied: Research into the child's attitude towards religion. *British Journal of Religious Education, 1,* 45–51.

Francis, L. J. (1979a). Research and the development of religious thinking. *Educational Studies, 5*, 109–115.

Francis, L. J. (1979b). School influence and pupil attitude towards religion. *British Journal of Educational Psychology, 49*, 107–123.

Francis, L. J. (1986a). *Partnership in Rural Education: Church schools and teacher attitudes.* London: Collins Liturgical Publications.

Francis, L. J. (1986b). Denominational schools and pupil attitude towards Christianity. *British Educational Research Journal, 12*, 145–152.

Francis, L. J. (1987a). Measuring attitudes towards Christianity among 12–18 year old pupils in Catholic schools. *Educational Research, 29*, 230–233.

Francis, L. J. (1987b). *Religion in the Primary School: Partnership between church and state?* London: Collins Liturgical Publications.

Francis, L. J. (1988). The development of a scale of attitude towards Christianity among 8–16 year olds. *Collected Original Resources in Education, 12*, fiche 1, A04.

Francis, L. J. (1989a). Measuring attitude towards Christianity during childhood and adolescence. *Personality and Individual Differences, 10*, 695–698.

Francis, L. J. (1989b). Drift from the churches: Secondary school pupils' attitudes towards Christianity. *British Journal of Religious Education, 11*, 76–86.

Francis, L. J. (1989c). Monitoring changing attitudes towards Christianity among secondary school pupils between 1974 and 1986. *British Journal of Educational Psychology, 59*, 86–91.

Francis, L. J. (1990). The religious significance of denominational identity among eleven year old children in England. *Journal of Christian Education, 97*, 23–28.

Francis, L. J. (1991a). Personality and attitude towards religion among adult church-goers in England. *Psychological Reports, 69*, 791–794.

Francis, L. J. (1991b). The personality characteristics of Anglican ordinands: Feminine men and masculine women? *Personality and Individual Differences, 12*, 1133–1140.

Francis, L. J. (1992a). Reliability and validity of the Francis Scale of Attitude towards Christianity (adult). *Panorama, 4*(1), 17–19.

Francis, L. J. (1992b). Reliability and validity of a short measure of attitude towards Christianity among nine to eleven year old pupils in England. *Collected Original Resources in Education, 16*(1), fiche 3, A02.

Francis, L. J. (1992c). Is psychoticism really the dimension of personality fundamental to religiosity? *Personality and Individual Differences, 13*, 645–652.

Francis, L. J. (1992d), Monitoring attitude towards Christianity: The 1990 study. *British Journal of Religious Education, 14*, 178–182.

Francis, L. J. (1992e). Male and female clergy in England: Their personality differences, gender reversal? *Journal of Empirical Theology, 5*, 31–38.

Francis, L. J. (1993a). Reliability and validity of a short scale of attitude towards Christianity among adults. *Psychological Reports, 72*, 615–618.

PSYCHOLOGICAL PERSPECTIVES ON RELIGIOUS EDUCATION

Francis, L. J. (1993b). Personality and religion among college students in the UK. *Personality and Individual Differences, 14,* 619–622.

Francis, L. J. (1993c). The dual nature of the Eysenckian neuroticism scales: A question of sex differences? *Personality and Individual Differences, 15,* 43–59.

Francis, L. J. (1996). The development of an abbreviated form of the Revised Junior Eysenck Personality Questionnaire (JEPQR-A) among 13- to 15-year-olds. *Personality and Individual Differences, 21,* 835–844.

Francis, L. J. (1997). The psychology of gender differences in religion: A review of empirical research. *Religion, 27,* 81–96.

Francis, L. J. (1998). The relationship between intelligence and religiosity among 15- to 16-year-olds. *Mental Health, Religion and Culture, 1,* 185–196.

Francis, L. J. (1999). Personality and attitude toward Christianity among undergraduates. *Journal of Research on Christian Education, 8,* 179–195.

Francis, L. J. (2001). Christianity and dogmatism revisited: A study among fifteen and sixteen year olds in the UK. *Religious Education, 96,* 211–226.

Francis, L. J. (2005a). Gender role orientation and attitude toward Christianity: A study among older men and women in the United Kingdom. *Journal of Psychology and Theology, 33,* 179–186.

Francis, L. J. (2005b). *Faith and psychology: Personality, religion and the individual.* London: Darton, Longman and Todd.

Francis, L. J. (2006). Attitude toward Christianity and premarital sex. *Psychological Reports, 98,* 140.

Francis, L. J. (2007). Introducing the New Indices of Religious Orientation (NIRO): Conceptualisation and measurement. *Mental Health, Religion and Culture, 10,* 585–602.

Francis, L. J. (2009). Understanding the attitudinal dimensions of religion and spirituality. In M. De Souza, L. J. Francis, J. O'Higgins-Norman, & D. G. Scott (Eds.), *International Handbook of education for spirituality, care and wellbeing* (pp. 147–167). Dordrecht: Springer.

Francis, L. J. (2010). Five loaves and two fishes: An empirical study in psychological type and biblical hermeneutics among Anglican preachers. *HTS Theological Studies, 66*(1), article #811, 1–5.

Francis, L. J. (2012a). What happened to the fig tree? An empirical study in psychological type and biblical hermeneutics. *Mental Health, Religion and Culture, 15,* 873–891.

Francis, L. J. (2012b). Interpreting and responding to the Johannine feeding narrative: An empirical study in the SIFT hermeneutical method among Anglican ministry training candidates. *HTS Theological Studies, 68*(1), article #1205, 1–9.

Francis, L. J. (2013). Ordinary readers and reader perspective on sacred texts: Drawing on empirical theology and Jungian psychology. In J. Astley and L. J. Francis (Eds.),

Exploring ordinary theology: Dimensions of everyday Christian existence and the life of the Church (pp. 87–96). Farnham: Ashgate.

Francis, L. J. (2015a). Taking discipleship learning seriously: Setting priorities for the rural church. *Rural Theology, 13*, 18–30.

Francis, L. J. (2015b). Footwashing and diaconal ordination. In J. Vincent (Ed.), *The Farewell Discourses in practice* (pp. 21–28). Blandford Forum: Deo Publishing.

Francis, L. J. (in press). Parental and peer influence on church attendance among adolescent Anglicans in England and Wales. *Journal of Anglican Studies.*

Francis, L. J., & ap Sion, T. (2013). A "Church" of Implicit Religion? A study in psychological type theory and measurement. *Implicit Religion, 16*(2), 169–189.

Francis, L. J., & ap Siôn, T. (2016a). Empirical theology and biblical hermeneutics: Exploring lessons for discipleship from the Road to Emmaus (Luke 24: 13–35). *Journal of Empirical Theology, 29*, 24–44.

Francis, L. J., & ap Siôn, T. (2016b). Jesus, psychological type and conflict: A study in biblical hermeneutics applying the reader perspective and SIFT approach to Mark 11: 11–21. *HTS Theological Studies, 72*(4), 1–9.

Francis, L. J., & ap Siôn, T. (2017). Reading the Lucan call of the first disciples differently: The voices of sensing and intuition. *Journal of Beliefs and Values, 38*, 188–198.

Francis, L. J., & ap Siôn, T. (2019). *The journey from educational research to classroom practice.* (https://warwick.ac.uk/fac/soc/ces/research/wreru/forschools/about/background).

Francis, L. J., ap Siôn, T., Lewis, C. A., Robbins, M., & Barnes, L. P. (2006). Attitude toward Christianity and religious experience: Replication among 16- to 18-year-old adolescents in Northern Ireland. *Research in Education, 76*, 56–61.

Francis, L. J., ap Siôn, T., McKenna, U., & Penny, G. (2017). Does Religious Education as an examination subject work to promote community cohesion? An empirical enquiry among 14- to 15-year-old adolescents in England and Wales. *British Journal of Religious Education, 39*, 303–316.

Francis, L. J., ap Sion, T., & Penny, G. (2014). Is belief in God a matter of public concern in contemporary Wales? An empirical enquiry concerning religious diversity among 13- to 15-year-old males. *Contemporary Wales, 27*, 40–57.

Francis, L. J., Astley, J., & McKenna, U. (2018). Belief in God, belief in science: Exploring the psychological correlates of fundamentalism as implicit religion. *Implicit Religion, 21*, 383–412.

Francis, L. J., Astley, J., & McKenna, U. (2019). Science disproves the biblical account of creation: Exploring the predictors of perceived conflict between science and religion among 13- to 15-year-old students. *British Journal of Religious Education, 41*, 188–201.

Francis, L. J., Athwal, S., & McKenna, U. (under review). Assessing attitude toward Sikhism: The psychometric properties of the Athwal-Francis Scale among Sikh adolescents.

PSYCHOLOGICAL PERSPECTIVES ON RELIGIOUS EDUCATION

Francis, L. J. & Atkins, P. (2000). *Exploring Luke's Gospel: A guide to the gospel readings in the Revised Common Lectionary*. London: Mowbray.

Francis, L. J. & Atkins, P. (2001). *Exploring Matthew's Gospel: A guide to the gospel readings in the Revised Common Lectionary*. London: Mowbray.

Francis, L. J. & Atkins, P. (2002). *Exploring Mark's Gospel: An aid for readers and preachers using year B of the Revised Common Lectionary*. London: Continuum.

Francis, L. J., & Bennett, G. A. (1992). Personality and religion among female drug misusers. *Drug and Alcohol Dependence, 30*, 27–31.

Francis, L. J., & Bourke, R. (2003). Personality and religion: Applying Cattell's model among secondary school pupils. *Current Psychology, 22*, 125–137.

Francis, L. J., Brockett, A., & Village, A. (2013). Measuring attitude toward theistic religion: Assessing the Astley-Francis Scale among Christian, Muslim and secular youth in England. *Research in Education, 89*, 70–81.

Francis, L. J., & Carter, M. (1980). Church aided secondary schools, religious education as an examination subject and pupil attitudes towards religion. *British Journal of Educational Psychology, 50*, 297–300.

Francis, L. J., & Casson, A. (2019). Retaining young Catholics in the Church: Assessing the importance of parental example. *Journal of Religious Education, 67*, 1–16.

Francis, L. J., Clymo, J., & Robbins, M. (2014). Fresh Expressions: Reaching those psychological types conventional forms of church find it hard to reach? *Practical Theology, 7*(4), 252–267.

Francis, L. J., & Craig, C. L. (2006). Tweenagers in the Church: An empirical perspective on attitude development. *Journal of Beliefs and Values, 27*, 95–109.

Francis, L. J., & Crea, G. (under review). The psychometric properties of the Italian translation of the Astley-Francis Scale of Attitude toward Theistic Faith: A study across the age range 13- to 80-years.

Francis, L. J., Croft, J., & Pyke, A. (2012). Religious diversity, empathy and God images: Perspectives from the psychology of religion and empirical theology shaping a study among adolescents in the UK. *Journal of Beliefs and Values, 33*, 293–307.

Francis, L. J., Croft, J., Pyke, A., & Robbins, M. (2012). Young people's attitudes to religious diversity: Quantitative approaches from social psychology and empirical theology. *Journal of Beliefs and Values, 33*, 279–292.

Francis, L. J., & Datoo, F. A. (2012). Inside the mosque: A study in psychological type profiling. *Mental Health, Religion and Culture, 15*(10), 1037–1046.

Francis, L. J., Elken, A., & Robbins, M. (2012). The affective dimension of religion and personal happiness among students in Estonia. *Journal of Research in Christian Education, 21*, 84–90.

Francis, L. J., & Enger, T. (2002). The Norwegian translation of the Francis Scale of Attitude toward Christianity. *Scandinavian Journal of Psychology, 43*, 363–367.

Francis, L. J., & Fearn, M. (1999). Religion and personality: A study among A-level students. *Transpersonal Psychology Review, 3*(2), 26–30.

Francis, L. J., Fearn, M., & Lewis, C. A. (2005). The impact of personality and religion on attitudes toward alcohol among 16–18 year olds in Northern Ireland. *Journal of Religion and Health, 44*, 267–289.

Francis, L. J., Fulljames, P., & Gibson, H. M. (1992). Does creationism commend the gospel? A developmental study among 11–17 year olds. *Religious Education, 87*, 19–27.

Francis, L. J., & Gibson, H. M. (1992). Popular religious television and adolescent attitudes towards Christianity. In J. Astley and D. V. Day (Eds.), *The contours of Christian education* (pp. 369–381). Great Wakering: McCrimmons.

Francis, L. J., & Gibson, H. M. (1993a). Television, pop culture and the drift from Christianity during adolescence. *British Journal of Religious Education, 15*, 31–37.

Francis, L. J., & Gibson, H. M. (1993b). Parental influence and adolescent religiosity: A study of church attendance and attitude towards Christianity among 11–12 and 15–16 year olds. *International Journal for the Psychology of Religion, 3*, 241–253.

Francis, L. J., Gibson, H. M., & Fulljames, P. (1990). Attitude towards Christianity, creationism, scientism and interest in science. *British Journal of Religious Education, 13*, 4–17.

Francis, L. J., Gibson, H. M., & Lankshear, D. W. (1991). The influence of Protestant Sunday Schools on attitudes towards Christianity among 11–15 year olds in Scotland. *British Journal of Religious Education, 14*, 35–42.

Francis, L. J., & Greer, J. E. (1990a). Measuring attitudes towards Christianity among pupils in Protestant secondary schools in Northern Ireland. *Personality and Individual Differences, 11*, 853–856.

Francis, L. J., & Greer, J. E. (1990b). Catholic schools and adolescent religiosity in Northern Ireland: Shaping moral values. *Irish Journal of Education, 24*, 40–47.

Francis, L. J., & Greer, J. E. (1993). The contribution of religious experience to Christian development: A study among fourth, fifth and sixth year pupils in Northern Ireland. *British Journal of Religious Education, 15*, 38–43.

Francis, L. J., & Greer, J. E. (1999). Attitude toward Christianity among secondary pupils in Northern Ireland: Persistence of denominational differences? *British Journal of Religious Education, 21*, 175–180.

Francis, L. J., & Greer, J. E. (2001). Shaping adolescents' attitudes toward science and religion in Northern Ireland: The role of scientism, creationism and denominational schools. *Research in Science and Technological Education, 19*, 39–53.

Francis, L. J., Greer, J. E. & Gibson, H. M. (1991). Reliability and validity of a short measure of attitude towards Christianity among secondary school pupils in England, Scotland and Northern Ireland. *Collected Original Resources in Education, 15*(3), fiche 2, G09.

Francis, L. J., & Hermans, C. A. M. (2000). Internal consistency reliability and construct validity of the Dutch translation of the Francis Scale of Attitude toward Christianity among adolescents. *Psychological Reports, 86*, 301–307.

Francis, L. J., & Hermans, C. A. M. (2009). Psychological health and attitude toward Christianity: A study among pupils attending Catholic schools in the Netherlands. *Journal of Religious Education, 57*, 47–58.

Francis, L. J., Hills, P., Schludermann, E., & Schludermann, S. (2008). Religion, psychological well-being and pe+rsonality: A study among undergraduate students in Canada. *Research in the Social Scientific Study of Religion, 19*, 1–16.

Francis, L. J., Ispas, D., Robbins, M., Ilie A., & Iliescu, D. (2009). The Romanian translation of the Francis Scale of Attitude toward Christianity: Internal consistency reliability, re-test reliability and construct validity among undergraduate students within a Greek Orthodox culture. *Pastoral Psychology, 58*, 49–54.

Francis, L. J., & Jewell, A. (1992). Shaping adolescent attitude towards the church: Comparison between Church of England and county secondary schools. *Evaluation and Research in Education, 6*, 13–21.

Francis, L. J., & Jones, S. H. (2011). Reading and proclaiming the resurrection: An empirical study in psychological type theory among ministry training and experienced preachers employing Mark 16 and Matthew 28. *Journal of Empirical Theology, 24*, 1–18.

Francis, L. J. & Jones, S. H. (2014). Life in the eucharistic community: An empirical study in psychological type theory and biblical hermeneutics reading John 6: 5–15. *Pastoral Psychology, 63*, 281–290.

Francis, L. J., & Jones, S. H. (2015a). An empirical approach to Mark's account of discipleship: Conversation between the Word of God and the People of God. *Rural Theology, 13*, 69–81.

Francis, L. J., & Jones, S. H. (2015b). Preparing for Disability Awareness Sunday: An educational exercise drawing on psychological perspectives for biblical hermeneutics. *International Journal of Christianity and Education, 19*, 197–214.

Francis, L. J., Jones, S. H., & Hebden, K. (2019). Binding and loosing on earth: Evaluating the strategy for church disciplinary procedures proposed in Matthew 18: 15–18 through the lenses of thinking and feeling. *HTS Theological Studies, 75*(3), article 5474, 1–10.

Francis, L. J., Jones, S. H., & Martinson, J. (2019). Exploring the Marcan account of the Baptism of Jesus through psychological lenses: An empirical study within a Black-led Black-majority Pentecostal church. *Journal of the European Pentecostal Theology Association, 39*, 100–115.

Francis, L. J., Jones, S. H., & Wilcox, C. (1997). Religiosity and dimensions of psychological well-being among 16–19 year olds. *Journal of Christian Education, 40*(1), 15–20.

Francis, L. J., Jones, S. H., & Wilcox, C. (2000). Religiosity and happiness: During adolescence, young adulthood and later life. *Journal of Psychology and Christianity, 19*, 245–257.

Francis, L. J., Kamble, S. V., & Robbins, M. (2016). The internal consistency reliability and construct validity of the Santosh-Francis Scale of Attitude toward Hinduism among students in India. *Mental Health, Religion and Culture, 19*, 476–483.

Francis, L. J., & Katz, Y. J. (2002). Religiosity and happiness: A study among Israeli female undergraduates. *Research in the Social Scientific Study of Religion, 13*, 75–86.

Francis, L. J, & Katz, Y. J. (2007). Measuring attitude toward Judaism: The internal consistency reliability of the Katz-Francis Scale of Attitude toward Judaism. *Mental Health, Religion and Culture, 10*, 309–324.

Francis, L. J., Katz, Y. J., Yablon, Y., & Robbins, M. (2004). Religiosity, personality and happiness: A study among Israeli male undergraduates. *Journal of Happiness Studies, 5*, 315–333.

Francis, L. J., & Kerr, S. (2003). Personality and religion among secondary school pupils in South Africa in the early 1990s. *Religion and Theology: A journal of contemporary religious discourse, 10*, 224–236.

Francis, L. J., Kerr, S., & Lewis, C. A. (2005). Assessing attitude toward Christianity among adolescents in South Africa: The Francis scale. *South African Journal of Psychology, 35*, 147–155.

Francis, L. J., & Kwiran, M. (1999a). Werthaltungen (einstellungen) gegenüber dem christentum bei deutschen heranwachsenden: Die Francis-Skala [Assessing attitude toward Christianity among German young people: The Francis Scale]. *Braunschweiger Beiträge, 89*(3), 50–54.

Francis, L. J., & Kwiran, M. (1999b). Personality and religion among secondary pupils in Germany. *Panorama, 11*, 34–44.

Francis, L. J., & Lankshear, D. W. (under review). Psychological type, temperament theory, and religious motivation: Exploring the distinctive congregational profile of Southwark Cathedral.

Francis, L. J., Lankshear, D. W., & Eccles, E. L. (2017). The internal consistency reliability and construct validity of the Francis Scale of Attitude toward Christianity among 8- to 11-year-old students in Wales. *Mental Health, Religion and Culture, 20*, 922–929.

Francis, L. J., Lankshear, D. W., & Eccles, E. L. (in press). Assessing student attitude toward Christianity in Church in Wales primary schools: Does aided status make a difference? *British Journal of Religious Education.*

Francis, L. J., Lankshear, D. W., Eccles, E. L., & McKenna, U. (2019). Sustaining church-going young Anglicans in England and Wales: Assessing influence of the home. *Journal of Beliefs and Values*, online first.

Francis, L. J., Lankshear, D. W., & Pearson, P. R. (1989). The relationship between religiosity and the short form JEPQ (JEPQ-S) indices of E, N, L and P among eleven year olds. *Personality and Individual Differences, 10*, 763–769.

PSYCHOLOGICAL PERSPECTIVES ON RELIGIOUS EDUCATION

Francis, L. J., Laycock, P., & Brewster, C. (2017). Exploring the factor structure of the Francis Psychological Type Scales (FPTS) among a sample of Anglican clergy in England. *Mental Health, Religion and Culture, 20*, 930–941.

Francis, L. J., & Lester, D. (1997). Religion, personality and happiness. *Journal of Contemporary Religion, 12*, 81–86.

Francis, L. J., & Lewis, C. A. (2016a). Internal consistency reliability and construct validity of the Astley-Francis Scale of Attitude toward Theistic Faith among religiously unaffiliated Christian and Muslim youth in the UK. *Mental Health, Religion and Culture, 19*, 484–492.

Francis, L. J., & Lewis, C. A. (2016b). Personal happiness and religious affect: An empirical enquiry among 16- to 19-year-old students in the Republic of Ireland. *Spirituality of a Personality, 3*(72), 98–116.

Francis, L. J., Lewis, C. A., & McKenna, U. (2017). Spirituality and empathy: A study among religiously unaffiliated adolescents within the UK. *Spirituality of a Personality, 3*(78), 325–345.

Francis, L. J., Lewis, C. A., & Ng, P. (2002). Assessing attitude toward Christianity among Chinese speaking adolescents in Hong Kong: The Francis scale. *North American Journal of Psychology, 4*, 431–440.

Francis, L. J., Lewis, C. A., & Ng, P. (2003). Psychological health and attitude toward Christianity among secondary school pupils in Hong Kong. *Journal of Psychology in Chinese Societies, 4*, 231–245.

Francis, L. J., Lewis, J. M., Brown, L. B., Philipchalk, R., & Lester, D. (1995). Personality and religion among undergraduate students in the United Kingdom, United States, Australia and Canada. *Journal of Psychology and Christianity, 14*, 250–262.

Francis, L. J., Lewis, J. M., Philipchalk, R., Brown, L. B., & Lester, D. (1995). The internal consistency reliability and construct validity of the Francis Scale of Attitude toward Christianity (adult) among undergraduate students in the UK, USA, Australia and Canada. *Personality and Individual Differences, 19*, 949–953.

Francis, L. J., Lewis, J. M., Philipchalk, R., Lester, D., & Brown, L. B. (1995). Reliability and validity of a short scale of attitude toward Christianity among students in the UK, USA, Australia and Canada. *Psychological Reports, 77*, 431–434.

Francis, L. J., & McCarron, M. M. (1989). The measurement of attitudes towards Christianity among Nigerian secondary school students. *Journal of Social Psychology, 129*, 569–571.

Francis, L. J., & McKenna, U. (2017a). Assessing attitude toward religious diversity among Muslim adolescents in the UK: The effect of religious and theological factors. *Journal of Beliefs and Values, 38*, 328–340.

Francis, L. J., & McKenna, U. (2017b). Muslim attitude toward freedom of religious clothing and symbols in schools within the UK: The effect of religious and theological factors. *Religione e Società, 32*, 50–58.

Francis, L. J., & McKenna, U. (2017c). The religious and social correlates of Muslim identity: An empirical enquiry into religification among male adolescents in the UK. *Oxford Review of Education, 43,* 550–565.

Francis, L. J., & McKenna, U. (2018). The experience of victimisation among Muslim adolescents in the UK: The effect of psychological and religious factors. *Religions, 9,* 243, 1–15.

Francis, L. J., & McKenna, U. (2019). The experience of victimisation among Christian adolescents in the UK: The effect of psychological and religious factors. In U. Riegel, S. Heil, B. Kalbheim, & A. Unser (Eds.), *Understanding religion: Empirical perspectives in practical theology. (Essays in honour of Hans-Georg Ziebertz)* (pp. 55–78). Munster: Waxmann.

Francis, L. J., McKenna, U., & Arweck, E. (2019). Countering anti-Muslim attitudes among Christian and religiously unaffiliated 13- to 15-year-old students in England and Wales: Testing the contact hypothesis. *Journal of Beliefs and Values,* online first.

Francis, L. J., McKenna, U., & Sahin, A. (2018). Facing the issues raised in Psalm 1 through thinking and feeling: Applying the SIFT approach to biblical hermeneutics among Muslim educators. *Religions, 9*(323), 1–11.

Francis, L. J., & Montgomery, A. (1992). Personality and attitudes towards Christianity among eleven to sixteen year old girls in a single sex Catholic school. *British Journal of Religious Education, 14,* 114–119.

Francis, L. J., Ok, U., & Robbins, M. (2017). Religion and happiness: A study among university students in Turkey. *Journal of Religion and Health, 56,* 1335–1347.

Francis, L. J. & Payne, V. J. (2002). The Payne Index of Ministry Styles (PIMS): Ministry styles and psychological type among male Anglican clergy in Wales. *Research in the Social Scientific Study of Religion, 13,* 125–141.

Francis, L. J., & Pearson, P. R. (1985a). Psychoticism and religiosity among 15 year olds. *Personality and Individual Differences, 6,* 397–398.

Francis, L. J., & Pearson, P. R. (1985b). Extraversion and religiosity. *Journal of Social Psychology, 125,* 269–270.

Francis, L. J., & Pearson, P. R. (1987). Empathic development during adolescence: Religiosity, the missing link? *Personality and Individual Differences, 8,* 145–148.

Francis, L. J., & Pearson, P. R. (1988). Religiosity and the short-scale EPQ-R indices of E, N and L, compared with the JEPI, JEPQ and EPQ. *Personality and Individual Differences, 9,* 653–657.

Francis, L. J., & Pearson, P. R. (1991). Religiosity, gender and the two faces of neuroticism. *Irish Journal of Psychology, 12,* 60–68.

Francis, L. J., Pearson, P. R., Carter, M., & Kay, W. K. (1981a). The relationship between neuroticism and religiosity among English 15- and 16-year olds. *Journal of Social Psychology, 114,* 99–102.

PSYCHOLOGICAL PERSPECTIVES ON RELIGIOUS EDUCATION

Francis, L. J., Pearson, P. R., Carter, M., & Kay, W. K. (1981b). Are introverts more religious? *British Journal of Social Psychology*, *20*, 101–104.

Francis, L. J., Pearson, P. R., & Kay, W. K. (1983a). Neuroticism and religiosity among English school children. *Journal of Social Psychology*, *121*, 149–150.

Francis, L. J., Pearson, P. R., & Kay, W. K. (1983b). Are introverts still more religious? *Personality and Individual Differences*, *4*, 211–212.

Francis, L. J., Pearson, P. R., & Lankshear, D. W. (1990). The relationship between social class and attitude towards Christianity among ten and eleven year old children. *Personality and Individual Differences*, *11*, 1019–1027.

Francis, L. J., & Penny, G. (2014). Gender difference in religion. In V. Saroglou (Ed.), *Religion, personality, and social behavior* (pp. 313–317). New York: Psychology Press.

Francis, L. J., & Penny, G. (2017). The personal and social significance of diverse religious affiliation in multi-faith London. In E. Arweck (Ed.), *Young people's attitudes to religious diversity* (pp. 222–241). London: Routledge.

Francis, L. J., Penny, G., & ap Siôn, T. (2017). Schools with a religious character and community cohesion in Wales. In E. Arweck (Ed.), *Young people's attitudes to religious diversity* (pp. 204–221). London: Routledge.

Francis, L. J., Penny, G., & Barnes, P. (2017). Testing the 'worlds apart' thesis: Catholic and Protestant schools in Northern Ireland. In E. Arweck (Ed.), *Young people's attitudes to religious diversity* (pp. 170–185). London: Routledge.

Francis, L. J., Penny, G., & McKenna, U. (2017). Does RE work and contribute to the common good in England? In E. Arweck (Ed.), *Young people's attitudes to religious diversity* (pp. 153–165). London: Routledge.

Francis, L. J., Penny, G., & Neil, P. (2017). Growing up Catholic in Scotland: Not one Catholic community but three. In E. Arweck (Ed.), *Young people's attitudes to religious diversity* (pp. 186–203). London: Routledge.

Francis, L. J., Penny, G., & Powell, R. (2018). Assessing peer and parental influence on the religious attitudes and attendance of young churchgoers: Exploring the Australian National Church Life Survey. *Journal of Beliefs and Values*, *39*, 57–72.

Francis, L. J., Penny, G., & Pyke, A. (2013). Young atheists' attitudes toward religious diversity: A study among 13- to 15-year-old males in the UK. *Theo-web: Zeitschrift für Religionspädagogik*, *12*(1), 57–78.

Francis, L. J., Pyke, A., & Penny, G. (2015). Christian affiliation, Christian practice, and attitudes to religious diversity: A quantitative analysis among 13- to 15-year-old female students in the UK. *Journal of Contemporary Religion*, *30*, 249–263.

Francis, L. J., Quesnell, M., & Lewis, C. A. (2010). Assessing attitude toward Christianity among adolescents in the Czech Republic: The Francis scale. *Irish Journal of Psychology*, *31*, 125–134.

Francis, L. J., & Robbins, M. (2000). Religion and happiness: A study in empirical theology. *Transpersonal Psychology Review*, *4*, 17–22.

Francis, L. J., & Robbins, M. (2003). Christianity and dogmatism among undergraduate students. *Journal of Beliefs and Values, 24*, 89–95.

Francis, L. J., & Robbins, M. (2015). Learning styles and psychological preferences among Christian disciples. *Rural Theology, 13*, 54–68.

Francis, L. J., Robbins, M., & Craig, C. L. (2011). The psychological type profile of Anglican churchgoers in England: Compatible or incompatible with their clergy? *International Journal of Practical Theology, 15*(2), 243–259.

Francis, L. J., Robbins, M., Lewis, C. A., Quigley, C. F., & Wheeler, C. (2004). Religiosity and general health among undergraduate students: A response to O'Connor, Cobb and O'Connor (2003). *Personality and Individual Differences, 37*, 485–494.

Francis, L. J., Robbins, M., Santosh, R., & Bhanot, S. (2008). Religion and mental health among Hindu young people in England. *Mental Health, Religion and Culture, 11*, 341–347.

Francis, L. J., Robbins, M., & White, A. (2003). Correlation between religion and happiness: A replication. *Psychological Reports, 92*, 51–52.

Francis, L. J., & Ross, C. F. J. (2000). Personality type and quest orientation of religiosity. *Journal of Psychological Type, 55*, 22–25.

Francis, L. J., & Ross, C. F. J. (2018). Psychologically informed engagement with the Matthean pericopes on Pilate and Judas through Jungian lenses: The SIFT approach. *HTS Theological Studies, 74*(1), article 5179, 1–12.

Francis, L. J., Sahin, A., & Al-Failakawi, F. (2008). Psychometric properties of two Islamic measures among young adults in Kuwait: The Sahin-Francis Scale of Attitude toward Islam and the Sahin Index of Islamic Moral Values. *Journal of Muslim Mental Health, 3*, 9–24.

Francis, L. J., Santosh, R., Robbins, M., & Vij, S. (2008). Assessing attitude toward Hinduism: The Santosh-Francis Scale. *Mental Health, Religion and Culture, 11*, 609–621.

Francis, L. J., & Smith, G. (2012). Separating sheep from goats: Using psychological type theory in a preaching workshop on Matthew 25: 31–46. *Journal of Adult Theological Education, 9*, 175–191.

Francis, L. J., & Smith, G. (2013). Reading and proclaiming the Birth Narratives from Luke and Matthew: A study in empirical theology among curates and their training incumbents employing the SIFT method. *HTS Theological Studies, 69*(1), article 2001, 1–13.

Francis, L. J., & Smith, G. (2014). Reading and proclaiming the Advent call of John the Baptist: An empirical enquiry employing the SIFT method. *HTS Theological Studies, 70*(1), article 2718, 1–9.

Francis, L. J., & Smith, G. (2015). Exploring organised and visionary approaches to designing an Advent Fun Day in an educational setting. *International Journal of Christianity and Education, 19*, 57–72.

Francis, L. J., & Smith, G. (2016). Introverts and extraverts reflecting on the experience of parish ministry: Conversation between training incumbents and curates. *Journal of Research on Christian Education*, 25, 76–85.

Francis, L. J., & Smith, G. (2017). Learning relationships: Church of England curates and training incumbents applying the SIFT approach to the Road to Emmaus. *HTS Theological Studies*, 73(4), article 4546, 1–11.

Francis, L. J., & Smith, G. (2018). Difficult texts: Psalm 1. *Theology*, 121, 197–200.

Francis, L. J., Smith, G., & Corio, A. S. (2018). I hate them with perfect hatred: Exploring Psalm 139 through the Jungian lenses of sensing, intuition, feeling, and thinking. *HTS Theological Studies*, 74(1), article 5058, 1–9.

Francis, L. J., Smith, G., & Francis-Dehqani, G. (2017). The missionary journey of Mark 6 and the experience of ministry in today's world: An empirical study in biblical hermeneutics among Anglican clergy. *HTS Theological Studies*, 73(3), article 4560, 1–7.

Francis, L. J., Smith, G., & Francis-Dehqani, G. (2018). Empirical explorations into biblical theologies of grace: Employing the SIFT approach among Anglican clergy. *Journal of Psychology and Christianity*, 37, 217–234.

Francis, L. J., & Stubbs, M. T. (1987). Measuring attitudes towards Christianity: From childhood to adulthood. *Personality and Individual Differences*, 8, 741–743.

Francis, L. J., Tekke, M., & Robbins, M. (2016). The psychometric properties of the Sahin-Francis Scale of Attitude toward Islam Revised among Sunni students in Malaysia. *Mental Health, Religion and Culture*, 19, 433–439.

Francis, L. J., & Thomas, E. M. (2003). The reliability and validity of the Francis Scale of Attitude toward Christianity among Welsh speaking 9–11 year olds. *The Psychologist in Wales*, 16, 9–14.

Francis, L. J., & Village, A. (2008). *Preaching with all our souls*. London: Continuum.

Francis, L. J., & Village, A. (2014). Church schools preparing adolescents for living in a religiously diverse society: An empirical enquiry in England and Wales. *Religious Education*, 109(3), 264–283.

Francis, L. J., & Village, A. (2015a). Assessing outgroup prejudice among 13- to 15-year-old students attending Catholic and Protestant secondary schools in Northern Ireland: An empirical enquiry. *Irish Educational Studies*, 34, 265–279.

Francis, L. J., & Village, A. (2015b). Go and observe the sower: Seeing empirical theology at work. *Journal of Empirical Theology*, 28, 155–183.

Francis, L. J., & Village, A. (in press). Christian ethos secondary schools, parental church attendance and student attitude toward Christianity. Exploring connections in England and Wales. *British Journal of Religious Education*.

Francis, L. J., Village, A., McKenna, U., & Penny, G. (2018). Freedom of religion and freedom of religious clothing and symbols in school: Exploring the impact of church schools in a religiously diverse society. In H. G. Ziebertz & C. Sterkens (Eds.),

Religion and civil human rights in empirical perspective (pp. 157–175). Dordrecht: Springer.

Francis, L. J., Village, A., Penny, G., & Neil, P. (2014). Catholic schools and attitudes toward religious diversity: An empirical enquiry among 13- to 15-year-old students in Scotland. *Scottish Educational Review, 46*(2), 36–53.

Francis, L. J., & Wilcox, C. (1996). Religion and gender orientation. *Personality and Individual Differences, 20,* 119–121.

Francis, L. J., & Wilcox, C. (1998). Religiosity and femininity: Do women really hold a more positive attitude toward Christianity? *Journal for the Scientific Study of Religion, 37,* 462–469.

Francis, L. J., Wright, H., & Robbins, M. (2016). Temperament theory and congregation studies: Different types for different services? *Practical Theology, 9*(1), 29–45.

Francis, L. J., Wulff, K., & Robbins, M. (2008). The relationship between work-related psychological health and psychological type among clergy serving in The Presbyterian Church (USA). *Journal of Empirical Theology, 21*(2), 166–182.

Francis, L. J., Yablon, Y. B., & Robbins, M. (2014). Religion and happiness: A study among female undergraduate students in Israel. *International Journal of Jewish Education Research, 7,* 77–92.

Francis, L. J., Ziebertz, H.-G.,& Lewis, C. A. (2002). The psychometric properties of the Francis Scale of Attitude toward Christianity among German students. *Panorama, 14,* 153–162.

Francis, L. J., Ziebertz, H.-G., & Lewis, C. A. (2003). The relationship between religion and happiness among German students. *Pastoral Psychology, 51,* 273–281.

Fulljames, P. (1996). Science, creation and Christianity: A further look. In L. J. Francis, W. K. Kay, and W. S. Campbell (Eds.), *Research in religious education* (pp. 257–260). Leominster: Gracewing.

Fulljames, P., & Francis, L. J. (1987a). The measurement of attitudes towards Christianity among Kenyan secondary school students. *Journal of Social Psychology, 127,* 407–409.

Fulljames, P., & Francis, L. J. (1987b). Creationism and student attitudes towards science and Christianity. *Journal of Christian Education, 90,* 51–55.

Fulljames, P., & Francis, L. J. (2003). Creationism among people in Kenya and Britain. In S. Coleman and L. Carlin (Eds.), *The cultures of creationism: Anti-evolutionism in English-speaking countries* (pp. 165–173). Aldershot: Ashgate.

Fulljames, P., Gibson, H. M., & Francis, L. J. (1991). Creationism, scientism, Christianity and science: a study in adolescent attitudes. *British Educational Research Journal, 17,* 171–190.

Garrity, F. D. (1960). *A study of the attitude of some secondary modern school pupils towards religious education.* Unpublished M.Ed. dissertation, University of Manchester.

Gates, B. E. (1976). *Religion and the developing world of children and young people.* Unpublished Ph.D. dissertation, University of Lancaster.

General Synod (2019). *Growing faith: Churches, schools and households.* London: Church of England (GS2121).

Gibson, H. M. (1989a). Measuring attitudes towards Christianity among 11–16 year old pupils in non-denominational schools in Scotland. *Educational Research, 31,* 221–227.

Gibson, H. M. (1989b). Attitudes to religion and science among school children aged 11 to 16 years in a Scottish city. *Journal of Empirical Theology, 2,* 5–26.

Gibson, H. M., & Francis, L. J. (1989). Measuring attitudes towards Christianity among 11- to 16-year old pupils in Catholic schools in Scotland. *Educational Research, 31,* 65–69.

Gibson, H. M., Francis, L. J., & Pearson, P. R. (1990). The relationship between social class and attitude towards Christianity among fourteen and fifteen year old adolescents. *Personality and Individual Differences, 11,* 631–635.

Gillings, V., & Joseph, S. (1996). Religiosity and social desirability: Impression management and self-deceptive posivity. *Personality and Individual Differences, 21,* 1047–1050.

Gobbel, R., & Gobbel, G. (1986). *The Bible: A child's playground.* London: SCM.

Godin, A. (1968). Genetic development of the symbolic function: Meaning and limits of the works of Goldman. *Religious Education, 63,* 439–445.

Goldberg, L. R. (1990). An alternative 'description of personality': The Big Five Factor structure. *Journal of Personality and Social Psychology, 59,* 1216–1229.

Goldberg, L. R. (1992). The development of markers for the Big Five Factor structure. *Psychological Assessment, 4,* 26–42.

Goldman, R. J. (1964). *Religious thinking from childhood to adolescence.* London: Routledge and Kegan Paul.

Goldman, R. J. (1965). *Readiness for religion.* London: Routledge and Kegan Paul.

Greer, J. E. (1972). The child's understanding of creation. *Educational Review, 24,* 94–110.

Greer, J. E. (1980). Stages in the development of religious thinking. *British Journal of Religious Education, 3,* 24–28.

Greer, J. E. (1981). Religious attitudes and thinking in Belfast pupils. *Educational Research, 23,* 177–189.

Greer, J. E. (1983). A critical study of 'Thinking about the Bible'. *British Journal of Religious Education, 5,* 113–25.

Greer, J. E. (1985). Viewing 'the other side' in Northern Ireland: Openness and attitudes to religion among Catholic and Protestant adolescents. *Journal for the Scientific Study of Religion, 24,* 275–292.

Greer, J. E., & Francis, L. J., (1990). The religious profile of pupils in Northern Ireland: A comparative study of pupils attending Catholic and Protestant secondary schools. *Journal of Empirical Theology, 3*, 35–50.

Greer, J. E., & Francis, L. J. (1991). Measuring attitudes towards Christianity among pupils in Catholic Secondary schools in Northern Ireland. *Educational Research, 33*, 70–73.

Greer, J. E., & Francis, L. J. (1992). Religious experience and attitude towards Christianity among secondary school children in Northern Ireland. *Journal of Social Psychology, 132*, 277–279.

Guttman, L. (1944). A basis for scaling qualitative data. *American Sociological Review, 9*, 139–150.

Halama, P., Martos, T., Adamovová, L. (2010). Religiosity and wellbeing in Slovak and Hungarian student samples: The role of personality traits. *Studia Psychologica, 52*, 101–115.

Hamid, S. N., Robbins, M., Nadeem, T., & Khan, Z. (2016). The Sahin-Francis Scale of Attitude towards Islam: A study among students in Pakistan. *Journal of Empirical Theology, 29*, 190–200.

Hancock, L., Tiliopoulos, N, & Francis, L. J. (2010). Psychometric properties of the Francis Scale of Attitude to Christianity among Australian Christians. *Journal of Religious Education, 58*(4), 72–75.

Hoge, D. R., & Petrillo, G. H. (1978). Development of religious thinking in adolescence: A test of Goldman's theories. *Journal for the Scientific Study of Religion, 17*, 139–154.

Hood Jr, R. W. (1978). The usefulness of indiscriminately pro and anti categories of religious orientation. *Journal for the Scientific Study of Religion, 17*, 419–431.

Hovemyr, M. (1998). The attribution of success and failure as related to different patterns of religious orientation. *International Journal for the Psychology of Religion, 8*, 107–124.

Howkins, K. G. (1966). *Religious thinking and religious education*. London: Tydale Press.

Hughes, J., Hewstone, M., Tausch, N., & Cairns, C. (2007). Prejudice, intergroup contact and identity: Do neighbourhoods matter? In M. Wetherell, M. Lafleche, & R. Berkeley (Eds.), *Identity, ethnic diversity and community cohesion* (pp. 102–112). London: Sage.

Hyde, K. E. (1968). A critique of Goldman's research. *Religious Education, 63*, 429–435.

Hyde, K. E. (1984). Twenty years after Goldman's research. *British Journal of Religious Education, 7*, 5–7.

Jaspard, J. M. (1971). The 6–12 year old child's representation of the Eucharistic presence. *Lumen Vitae, 26*, 237–262.

John Paul II. (1981). *Familiaris consortio* [The role of the Christian family in the modern world]. Retrieved from the Vatican website on 26th July 2017: http://w2.vatican.va/content/john-paul-ii/en/apost_exhortations/documents/hf_jp-ii_exh_19811122_familiaris-consortio.html.

PSYCHOLOGICAL PERSPECTIVES ON RELIGIOUS EDUCATION 79

Johnson, W. P. C. (1966). *The religious attitudes of secondary modern county school pupils*. Unpublished M.Ed. dissertation, University of Manchester.

Jones, D. L. (1997). *Measuring the dimensions of religion: The Batson and Ventis scales*. Unpublished master's dissertation, Westminster College Oxford.

Jones, J. A. (1962). *An investigation into the response of boys and girls to scripture as a school subject in certain co-educational grammar schools in industrial South Wales*. Unpublished M.A. dissertation, University of Wales (Swansea).

Jones, S. H., & Francis, L. J. (1996). Religiosity and self-esteem during childhood and adolescence. In L. J. Francis, W. K. Kay, and W. S. Campbell (Eds.), *Research in religious education* (pp. 189–206). Leominster: Fowler Wright Books.

Jones, S. H., & Francis, L. J. (1999). Personality type and attitude toward Christianity among student churchgoers. *Journal of Beliefs and Values, 20*, 105–109.

Jones, S. H., & Francis, L. J. (2019). Searching for the lost sheep (Matthew 18: 10–14): Do sensing types and intuitive types find different things? *Rural Theology, 17*, 74–92.

Jorm, A. F. (1987). Sex differences in neuroticism: A quantitative synthesis of published research. *Australian and New Zealand Journal of Psychiatry, 21*, 501–506.

Joseph, S., & Diduca, D. (2001). Schizotypy and religiosity in 13–18 year old school pupils. *Mental Health, Religion and Culture, 4*, 63–69. doi.org/10.1080/13674670124766.

Joseph, S., & Lewis, C. A. (1997). The Francis Scale of Attitude towards Christianity: Intrinsic or extrinsic religiosity? *Psychological Reports, 80*, 609–610.

Jung, C. G. (1971). *Psychological types: The collected works* (volume 6). London: Routledge and Kegan Paul.

Kay, W. K. (1981a). Psychoticism and attitude to religion. *Personality and Individual Differences, 2*, 249–252.

Kay, W. K. (1981b). Conversion among 11–15 year olds. *Spectrum, 13*(2), 26–33.

Kay, W. K. (1981c). Marital happiness and children's attitudes to religion. *British Journal of Religious Education, 3*, 102–105.

Kay, W. K. (1981d). Syllabuses and attitudes to Christianity. *The Irish Catechist, 5*(2), 16–21.

Kay, W. K. (1981e). *Religious thinking, attitudes and personality amongst secondary pupils in England and Ireland*. Unpublished Ph.D. dissertation, University of Reading.

Kay, W. K., & Francis, L. J. (1996). *Drift from the churches: Attitude toward Christianity during childhood and adolescence*. Cardiff: University of Wales Press.

Kay, W. K., Francis, L. J., & Gibson, H. M. (1996). Attitude toward Christianity and the transition to formal operational thinking. *British Journal of Religious Education, 19*, 45–55.

Keirsey, D., & Bates, M. (1978). *Please understand me*. Del Mar, CA: Prometheus Nemesis.

Kille, D. A. (2001). *Psychological biblical criticism*. Minneapolis, MN: Fortress Press.

Kingam, B. A. (1969). *The study of some factors hindering religious education of a group of primary school children*. Unpublished M.Ed. dissertation, University of Liverpool.

Kosek, R. B. (1999). Adaptation of the Big Five as a hermeneutic instrument for religious constructs. *Personality and Individual Differences, 27*, 229–237.

Langdon, A. A. (1969). A critical examination of Dr Goldman's research study on religious thinking from childhood to adolescence. *Journal of Christian Education, 12*(1), 37–63.

Lankshear, D. W., & Francis, L. J. (2015). Inside Southwark Cathedral: A study in psychological type profiling. *Mental Health, Religion and Culture, 18*(8), 664–674.

Lesmana, C. B. J., Tiliopoulos, N., & Francis, L. J. (2011). The internal consistency reliability of the Santosh-Francis Scale of Attitude toward Hinduism among Balinese Hindus. *International Journal of Hindu Studies, 15*, 293–301.

Lester, D., & Francis, L. J. (1993). Is religiosity related to suicidal ideation after personality and mood are taken into account? *Personality and Individual Differences, 15*, 591–592.

Lewis, C. A. (1994). Religiosity and obsessionality: The relationship between Freud's 'religious practices'. *Journal of Psychology, 128*, 189–196.

Lewis, C. A. (1996). Religiosity and obsessionality. In L. J. Francis, W. K. Kay, and W. S. Campbell (Eds.), *Research in religious education* (pp. 219–227). Leominster: Gracewing.

Lewis, C. A. (1998). Towards a clarification of the association between religiosity and life satisfaction. *Journal of Beliefs and Values, 19*, 119–122.

Lewis, C. A. (1999). Is the relationship between religiosity and personality 'contaminated' by social desirability as assessed by the lie scale? A methodological reply to Michael W. Eysenck (1998). *Mental Health, Religion and Culture, 2*, 105–114.

Lewis, C. A. (2000). The religiosity-psychoticism relationship and the two factors of social desirability: A response to Michael W. Eysenck (1999). *Mental Health, Religion and Culture, 3*, 39–45.

Lewis, C. A., Adamovová, L., & Francis, L. J. (2008). Assessing the Francis Scale of Attitude toward Christianity among Slovak students. *International Journal of Psychology, 43*, 463.

Lewis, C. A., Cruise, S. M., & Lattimer, B. (2007). Temporal stability of the Francis Scale of Attitude toward Christianity short-form among 10- to 12-year-old English children: Test-retest data over 15 weeks. *Archive for the Psychology of Religion, 29*, 259–267.

Lewis, C. A., Cruise, S. M., & McGuckin, C. (2005). Temporal stability of the Francis Scale of Attitude toward Christianity short-form: Test-retest data over one week. *Psychological Reports, 96*, 266–268.

Lewis, C. A., Cruise, S. M., McGuckin, C., & Francis, L. J. (2006). Temporal stability of the Francis Scale of Attitude toward Christianity among 9- to 11-year-old English children: Test-retest data over six weeks. *Social Behaviour and Personality, 34*, 1081–1086.

PSYCHOLOGICAL PERSPECTIVES ON RELIGIOUS EDUCATION

Lewis, C. A., & Francis, L. J. (2000). Personality and religion among female university students in France. *International Journal of Psychology*, *35*, 229.

Lewis, C. A., & Francis, L. J. (2003). Evaluer l'attitude d'étudiantes universitaires françaises à l'égard du Christianisme: L'Echelle de Francis. [Assessing the attitude of French university students toward Christianity: The Francis scale] *Sciences Pastorals*, *22*, 179–190.

Lewis, C. A., & Francis, L. J. (2004). Reliability and validity of a French translation of a short scale of attitude toward Christianity. *Pastoral Psychology*, *52*, 459–464.

Lewis, C. A., & Francis, L. J. (2014). Personality and religion among female university students in France. *Psychology, Society and Education*, *6*(2), 68–81.

Lewis, C. A., & Joseph, S. (1994). Religiosity: Psychoticism and obsessionality in Northern Irish university students. *Personality and Individual Differences*, *17*, 685–687.

Lewis, C. A., Joseph, S., & Noble, K. E. (1996). Is religiosity associated with life satisfaction? *Psychological Reports*, *79*, 429–430.

Lewis, C. A., & Maltby, J. (1992). Religiosity and preoedipal fixation: A refinement. *Journal of Psychology*, *126*, 687–688.

Lewis, C. A., & Maltby, J. (1994). Religious attitudes and obsessional personality traits among UK adults. *Psychological Reports*, *75*, 353–354.

Lewis, C. A., & Maltby, J. (1995a). The reliability and validity of the Francis Scale of Attitude towards Christianity among US adults. *Psychological Reports*, *76*, 1243–1247.

Lewis, C. A., & Maltby, J. (1995b). Religiosity and personality among US adults. *Personality and Individual Differences*, *18*, 293–295.

Lewis, C. A., & Maltby, J. (1995c). Religious attitude and practice: The relationship with obsessionality. *Personality and Individual Differences*, *19*, 105–108.

Lewis, C. A., & Maltby, J. (1997). Reliability and validity of the Francis Scale of Attitude toward Christianity (adult) among Northern Irish university students. *Irish Journal of Psychology*, *18*, 349–354.

Lewis, C. A., & Maltby, J. (2000). Conservatism and attitude toward Christianity. *Personality and Individual Differences*, *29*, 793–798.

Lewis, C. A., Shevlin, M., Lloyd, N. S. V., & Adamson, G. (1998). The Francis Scale of Attitude toward Christianity (short scale): Exploratory and confirmatory factor analysis among English students. *Journal of Social Behaviour and Personality*, *13*, 167–175.

Lewis, C. A., Varvatsoulias, G., & Williams, E. (2012). Psychological type profile of practising Greek Orthodox churchgoers in London. *Mental, Health, Religion and Culture*, *15*(10), 979–986.

Lewis, J. M. (1974). *An examination of the attitudes of pupils towards the content and method of teaching religious education in certain co-educational comprehensive schools in Wales*. Unpublished M.Ed. dissertation, University of Wales, (Swansea).

Likert, R. (1932). A technique for the measurement of attitudes. *Archives of Psychology, 140,* 1–55.

Lumbroso, P., Fayn, K., Tiliopoulos, N., & Francis, L. J. (2016). The internal consistency reliability of the Katz-Francis Scale of Attitude toward Judaism among Australian Jews. *Religions, 7,* 123, 1–6.

Lytle, A. (2018). Intergroup contact theory: Recent developments and future directions. *Social Justice Research, 31,* 374–385.

Maas, R. M. (1985). Biblical catechesis and religious development: the Goldman project twenty years later. *Living Light, 22,* 124–144.

Maltby, J. (1994). The reliability and validity of the Francis Scale of Attitude towards Christianity among Republic of Ireland adults. *Irish Journal of Psychology, 15,* 595–598.

Maltby, J. (1995). Is there a denominational difference in scores on the Francis scale of attitude towards Christianity among Northern Irish adults? *Psychological Reports, 76,* 88–90.

Maltby, J. (1997a). Personality correlates of religiosity among adults in the Republic of Ireland. *Psychological Reports, 81,* 827–831.

Maltby, J. (1997b). Obsessional personality traits: The association with attitudes toward Christianity and religious puritanism. *Journal of Psychology, 131,* 675–677.

Maltby, J., & Day, L. (1998). Amending a measure of the Quest Religious Orientation: Applicability of the scale's use among religious and non-religious persons. *Personality and Individual Differences, 25,* 517–522.

Maltby, J., & Lewis, C. A. (1996). Measuring intrinsic and extrinsic orientation toward religion: Amendments for its use among religious and non-religious samples. *Personality and Individual Differences, 21,* 937–946.

Maltby, J., & Lewis, C. A. (1997). The reliability and validity of a short scale of attitude toward Christianity among USA, English, Republic of Ireland and Northern Ireland adults. *Personality and Individual Differences, 22,* 649–654.

Maltby, J., McCollam, P., & Millar, D. (1994). Religiosity and obsessionality: A refinement. *Journal of Psychology, 128,* 609–611.

Maselko, J., & Kubzansky, L. D. (2006). Gender differences in religious practices, spiritual experiences and health: Results from the US General Social Survey. *Social and Medicine, 62,* 2848–2860.

McGrady, A. G. (1982). Goldman: A Piagetian based critique. *The Irish Catechist, 6,* 19–29.

McGrady, A. G. (1983). Teaching the Bible: Research from a Piagetian perspective. *British Journal of Religious Education, 5,* 126–33.

McGrady, A. G. (1990). *The development of religious thinking: A comparison of metaphoric and operational paradigms.* Unpublished Ph.D. dissertation, University of Birmingham.

McGrady, A. G. (1994a). Metaphorical and operational aspects of religious thinking: Research with Irish Catholic pupils (part 1). *British Journal of Religious Education, 16*, 148–163.

McGrady, A. G. (1994b). Metaphorical and operational aspects of religious thinking: Research with Irish Catholic pupils (part 2). *British Journal of Religious Education, 17*, 56–62.

McKenna, U., & Francis, L. J. (2019). Growing up female and Muslim in the UK: An empirical enquiry into the distinctive religious and social values of young Muslims. *British Journal of Religious Education, 41*, 388–401.

McKenna, U., & Francis, L. J. (under review a). Testing the contact hypothesis in a post-truth era: Personal friendships with Sikhs countering anti-Sikh attitudes? In Z. Gross (Ed.), *Religious education in a multicultural post-truth era: International perspectives.* London: Springer.

McKenna, U., & Francis, L. J. (under review b). Testing the contact hypothesis: The association between personal friendships and anti-Jewish attitudes among 13- to 15-year-old students in England and Wales.

McKinney, S., Francis, L. J., & McKenna, U. (2019). Assessing sectarian attitudes among Catholic adolescents in Scotland: How responsible are Catholic schools? *Journal of Beliefs and Values,* online first.

Mehrabian, A., & Epstein, N. (1972). A measure of emotional empathy. *Journal of Personality, 40*, 525–543.

Mercer, C., & Durham, T. W. (1999). Religious mysticism and gender orientation. *Journal for the Scientific Study of Religion, 38*, 175–182.

Miles, G. B. (1971). *The study of logical thinking and moral judgements in GCE bible knowledge candidates.* Unpublished M.Ed. dissertation, University of Leeds.

Miranda-Tapia, G. A., Cogollo, Z., Herazo, E., & Campo-Arias, A. (2010). Stability of the Spanish version of the five-item Francis Scale of Attitude toward Christianity. *Psychological Reports, 107*, 949–952.

Morley, H. C. (1975). Religious concepts of slow learners: An application of the findings of Ronald Goldman. *Learning for Living, 14*, 107–110.

Moxy, A., McEvoy, M., & Bowe, S. (2011). Spirituality, religion, social support and health among older Australian adults. *Australasian Journal on Ageing, 30*, 82–88.

Munayer, S. J. (2000). *The ethnic identity of Palestinian Arab Christian adolescents in Israel.* Unpublished doctoral dissertation, University of Wales: Oxford Centre for Mission Studies.

Murphy, J. (1971). *Church, state and schools in Britain 1800–1970.* London: Routledge and Kegan Paul.

Murphy, R. J. L. (1977). The development of religious thinking in children in three easy stages? *Learning for Living, 17*, 16–19.

Murphy, R. J. L. (1979). *An investigation into some aspects of the development of religious thinking in children aged between 6 and 11 years*. Unpublished Ph.D. dissertation, University of St Andrews.

Musharraf, S., Lewis, C. A., & Sultan, S. (2014). The Urdu translation of the Sahin-Francis Scale of Attitude toward Islam: A case of using only positive valence items in Pakistan. *Journal of Beliefs and Values, 35*, 25–35.

Myers, I. B., & McCaulley, M. H. (1985). *Manual: A guide to the development and use of the Myers-Briggs Type Indicator*. Palo Alto, CA: Consulting Psychologists Press.

Nazar, N. P. (2019). Leslie Francis' scale of attitudes towards religion and its utilisation in Greek religious education. *Greek Journal of Religious Education, 2*, 87–102.

Nye, W. C., & Carlson, J. S. (1984). The development of the concept of God in children. *Journal of Genetic Psychology, 145*, 137–142.

Office for National Statistics (2012). *Religion in England and Wales 2011*. London: Office for National Statistics.

Ok, U. (2016). The Ok Religious Attitude Scale (Islam): Introducing an instrument originated in Turkish for international use. *Journal of Beliefs and Values, 37*, 55–67.

Osgood, C. E., Suci, G. J., & Tannenbaum, P. H. (1957). *The measurement of meaning*. Urbana, IL: University of Illinois Press.

Payne, V. J., Lewis, C. A., & Francis, L. J. (under review). Confirming the factor structure of the Francis Psychological Type Scales (FPTS) among a sample of Anglican clergy in Wales. *Pastoral Psychology*.

Pearson, P. R., Francis, L. J., & Lightbown, T. J. (1986). Impulsivity and religiosity. *Personality and Individual Differences, 7*, 89–94.

Peatling, J. H. (1973). *The incidence of concrete and abstract religious thinking in the interpretation of three bible stories by pupils enrolled in grades four through twelve in selected schools in the Episcopal Church in the United States of America*. Unpublished Ph.D. dissertation, University of New York.

Peatling, J. H. (1974). Cognitive development in pupils in grades four through twelve: The incidence of concrete and abstract religious thinking. *Character Potential, 7*(1), 52–61.

Peatling, J. H. (1977). On beyond Goldman: Religious thinking and the 1970s. *Learning for Living, 16*, 99–108.

Peatling, J. H., & Laabs, C. W. (1975). Cognitive development of pupils in grades four through twelve: A comparative study of Lutheran and Episcopalian children and youth. *Character Potential, 7*, 107–117.

Peatling, J. H., Laabs, C. W., & Newton, T. B. (1975). Cognitive development: A three sample comparison of means on the Peatling scale of religious thinking. *Character Potential, 7*, 159–162.

Penny, G., & Francis, L. J. (2014). Religion and self-esteem: A study among 13- to 15-year-old students in the UK. In J. H. Borders (Ed.) *Handbook on the psychology of self-esteem* (pp. 19–45). New York: Nova Science.

PSYCHOLOGICAL PERSPECTIVES ON RELIGIOUS EDUCATION

Penny, G., Francis, L. J., & Robbins, M. (2015). Why are women more religious than men? Testing the explanatory power of personality theory among undergraduate students in Wales. *Mental Health, Religion and Culture, 18*, 492–502.

Pettigrew, T. F. (1998). Intergroup contact theory. *Annual Review of Psychology, 49*, 65–85.

Petrovich, O. (1988). Re-review: Ronald Goldman's Religious Thinking from Childhood to Adolescence, *Modern Churchman, 30*(2), 44–49.

Piaget, J. (1969). *The child's conception of time*. London: Routledge and Kegan Paul.

Piaget, J. (1970). *The child's conception of movement and speed*. London: Routledge and Kegan Paul.

Piaget, J. (1972). *The principles of genetic epistemology*. London: Routledge and Kegan Paul.

Piaget, J. (1973). *The child's conception of the world*. London: Routledge and Kegan Paul.

Piedmont, R. L. (1999). Strategies for using the five-factor model of personality in religious research. *Journal of Psychology and Theology, 27*, 338–350.

Pollak G., & Pickel, D. (2007). Religious individualization or secularization? Testing hypotheses of religious change—the case of Eastern and Western Germany. *British Journal of Sociology, 58*, 603–632.

Povall, C. H. (1971). *Some factors affecting pupils' attitudes to religious education*. Unpublished M.Ed. dissertation, University of Manchester.

Rich, E. E. (1970). *The Education Act 1870*. London: Longmans.

Richmond, R. C. (1972). Maturity of religious judgements and differences of religious attitudes between ages of 13 and 16 years. *Educational Review, 24*, 225–230.

Robbins, M., & Francis, L. J. (1996). Are religious people happier? A study among undergraduates. In L. J. Francis, W. K. Kay, & W. S. Campbell (Eds.), *Research in religious education* (pp. 207–218). Leominster: Fowler Wright Books.

Robbins, M., & Francis, L. J. (2011). All are called, but some psychological types are more likely to respond: Profiling churchgoers in Australia. *Research in the Social Scientific Study of Religion, 22*, 213–229.

Robbins, M., & Francis, L. J. (2012). The psychological type profile of Australian Catholic congregations: Psychological theory and congregational studies. In A. W. Ata (Ed.), *Catholics and Catholicism in contemporary Australia: Challenges and achievements* (pp. 262–281). Melbourne, Victoria: David Lovell Publishing.

Robbins, M., Francis, L. J., & Gibbs, D. (1995). Personality and religion: A study among 8–11 year olds. *Journal of Beliefs and Values, 16*(1), 1–6.

Robbins, M., Francis, L. J., Haley, J. M., & Kay, W. K. (2001). The personality characteristics of Methodist ministers: Feminine men and masculine women? *Journal for the Scientific Study of Religion, 40*, 123–128.

Robbins, M., Francis, L. J., McIlroy, D., Clarke, R., & Pritchard, L. (2010). Three religious orientations and five personality factors: An exploratory study among adults in England. *Mental Health, Religion and Culture, 13*, 771–775.

Robbins, M., Francis, L. J., & Powell, R. (2012). Work-related psychological health among clergywomen in Australia. *Mental Health, Religion and Culture*, *15*(9), 933–944.

Robbins, M., Francis, L. J., & Rutledge, C. (1997). The personality characteristics of Anglican stipendiary parochial clergy in England: Gender differences revisited. *Personality and Individual Differences*, *23*, 199–204.

Robbins, M., Francis, L. J., & Williams, N. (2003). Reliability of the Francis Scale of Attitude toward Christianity among 8 year olds. *Psychological Reports*, *92*, 104.

Rocklin, T., & Revelle, W. (1981). The measurement of extraversion: A comparison of the Eysenck Personality Inventory and the Eysenck Personality Questionnaire. *British Journal of Social Psychology*, *20*, 279–284.

Rollins, W. G. (1999). *Soul and psyche: The Bible in psychological perspective*. Minneapolis, MN: Fortress Press.

Rollins, W. G., & Kille, D. A. (2007). *Psychological insight into the bible: Texts and readings*. Grand Rapids, MI: Eerdmans.

Roman, R. E., & Lester, D. (1999). Religiosity and mental health. *Psychological Reports*, *85*, 1088.

Rosenberg, M. (1965). *Society and the adolescent self-image*. Princeton, NJ: Princeton University Press.

Ross, C. F. J. (1992). The intuitive function and religious orientation. *Journal of Analytical Psychology*, *37*, 83–103.

Ross, C. F. J., & Francis, L. J. (2010). The relationship of intrinsic, extrinsic and quest religious orientations to Jungian psychological type among churchgoers in England and Wales. *Mental Health, Religion and Culture*, *13*, 805–819.

Rothbart, M., & John, O. P. (1985). Social categorization and behavioral episodes: A cognitive analysis of the effects of intergroup contact. *Journal of Social Issues*, *41*, 81–104.

Roy, P. R. (1979). *Applications of Piaget's theory of cognitive development to religious thinking, with special reference to the work of Dr R. G. Goldman*. Unpublished M.Ed. dissertation, University of Liverpool.

Russell, A. (1978). *The attitude of primary school children to religious education*. Unpublished M.Phil. dissertation, University of Nottingham.

Sahin, A., & Francis, L. J. (2002). Assessing attitude toward Islam among Muslim adolescents: The psychometric properties of the Sahin-Francis scale. *Muslim Education Quarterly*, *19*(4), 35–47.

Saroglou, V. (2002). Religion and the five factors of personality: A meta-analytic review. *Personality and Individual Differences*, *32*, 15–25.

Saroglou, V., & Muñoz-Garcia, A. (2008). Individual differences in religion and spirituality: An issue of personality traits and/or values. *Journal for the Scientific Study of Religion*, *47*, 83–101.

Schludermann, E. H., Schludermann, S. M., & Huynh, C.-L. (2000). Religiosity, prosocial values, and adjustment among students in Catholic high schools in Canada. *Journal of Beliefs and Values*, *21*, 99–115.

PSYCHOLOGICAL PERSPECTIVES ON RELIGIOUS EDUCATION

Schludermann, E. H., Schludermann, S. M., Needham, D., & Mulenga, M. (2001). Fear of rejection versus religious commitment as predictors of adjustment among Reformed and Evangelical college students in Canada. *Journal of Beliefs and Values*, 22, 209–224.

Segovia, F. F., & Tolbert, M. A. (Eds) (1995a). *Reading from this Place: social location and biblical interpretation in the United States*. Minneapolis, MN: Fortress Press.

Segovia, F. F., & Tolbert, M. A. (Eds) (1995b). *Readings from this Place: social location and biblical interpretation in global perspective*. Minneapolis, MN: Fortress Press.

Shuter-Dyson, R. (2000). Profiling music students: Personality and religiosity. *Psychology of Music*, 28, 190–196.

Slee, N. M. (1986a). Goldman yet again: An overview and critique of his contribution to research. *British Journal of Religious Education*, 8, 84–93.

Slee, N. M. (1986b). A note on Goldman's methods of data analysis with special reference to scalogram analysis. *British Journal of Religious Education*, 8, 168–175.

Slee, N. M. (1990). Getting away from Goldman: Changing perspectives on the development of religious thinking. *Modern Churchman*, 32(1), 1–9.

Smith, C., Denton, M. L., Faris, R., & Regenerus, M. (2002). Mapping American adolescent participation. *Journal for the Scientific Study of Religion*, 41, 597–612.

Smith, G. (2015a). Psychological type and the training relationship: An empirical study among curates and training incumbents. *Mental Health, Religion and Culture*, 18, 556–565.

Smith, G. (2015b). The work-related psychological health of introverts and extraverts in ministry: Exploring the balanced affect model. *Research in the Social Scientific Study of Religion*, 26, 155–165.

Smith, G. (2018). Valuing the learning style of curates: Implications for training ministers. *Rural Theology*, 16, 123–131.

Smith, G., & Francis, L. J. (2015). Experiencing and reflecting on thinking and feeling in pastoral care: Deploying psychological type theory in continuing ministerial formation. *Journal of Adult Theological Education*, 12, 69–78.

Smith, G., & Francis, L. J. (2016). Difficult texts: Mark 10: 46–52. *Theology*, 119, 200–203.

Smith, R. D. (1990). Religious orientation, sex-role traditionalism, and gender identity: Contrasting male and female responses to socializing forces. *Sociological Analysis*, 51, 377–385.

Stiefel, R. E. (1992). Preaching to all the people: The use of Jungian typology and the Myers-Briggs Type Indicator in the teaching of preaching and in the preparation of sermons. *Anglican Theological Review*, 72, 175–202.

Swindells, T., Francis, L. J., & Robbins, M. (2010). Shaping attitude toward Christianity among year seven pupils: The influence of sex, church, home and primary school. *Journal of Beliefs and Values*, 311, 343–348.

Tamminen, K. (1976). Research concerning the development of religious thinking in Finnish students. *Character Potential*, 7, 206–219.

Tamminen, K. (1991). *Religious development in childhood and youth: An empirical study.* Helsinki: Suomalainen Tiedeakatemia.

Taylor, A., & MacDonald, D. A. (1999). Religion and the five factor model of personality: an exploratory investigation using a Canadian university sample. *Personality and Individual Differences, 27,* 1243–1259.

Taylor, H. P. (1970). *A comparative study of the religious attitudes, beliefs and practices of sixth formers in Anglican, state and Roman Catholic schools and an assessment of religious opinion upon them asserted by home and school.* Unpublished M.Phil. dissertation, University of London.

Tekke, M., Francis, L. J., & Robbins, M. (2018). Religious affect and personal happiness: A replication among Sunni students in Malaysia. *Journal of Muslim Mental Health, 11*(2), 3–15.

Thompson, E. H. (1991). Beneath the status characteristics: Gender variations in religiousness. *Journal for the Scientific Study of Religion, 30,* 381–394.

Thurstone, L. L. (1928). Attitudes can be measured. *American Journal of Sociology, 33,* 529–554.

Tiliopoulos, N., Francis, L. J., & Jiang, Y. (2013). The Chinese translation of the Francis Scale of Attitude toward Christianity: Factor structure, internal consistency reliability and construct validity among Protestant Christians in Shanghai. *Pastoral Psychology, 62,* 75–79.

Tiliopoulos, N., Francis, L. J., & Slattery, M. (2010). The internal consistency reliability of the Santosh-Francis Scale of Attitude toward Hinduism among Bunts in South India. *North American Journal of Psychology, 12,* 185–190.

Tiliopoulos, N., Francis, L. J., & Slattery, M. (2011). The affective dimension of religion and happiness among Hindu Bunts in South India. *Transpersonal Psychology Review, 14,* 25–29.

Tjeltveit, A. C., Fiordalisi, A. M., & Smith, C. (1996). Relationships among mental health values and various dimensions of religiousness. *Journal of Social and Clinical Psychology, 15,* 364–377.

Turner, E. B. (1970). *Religious understanding and religious attitudes in male urban adolescents.* Unpublished Ph.D. dissertation, The Queen's University of Belfast.

Van Bunnen, C. (1965). The burning bush: The symbolic implications of a bible story among children from 5–12 years. In A. Godin (Ed.), *From religious experience to a religious attitude* (pp. 171–182). Chicago, IL: Loyola University Press.

Vezzali L., & Stathi, S. (Ed.) (2017). *Intergroup contact theory: Recent developments and future directions.* Abingdon: Routledge.

Village, A. (2011). Gifts differing? Psychological type among stipendiary and non-stipendiary clergy. *Research in the Social Scientific Study of Religion, 22,* 230–250.

Village, A. (2015). Who goes there? Attendance at Fresh Expressions of Church in relation to psychological type preference among readers of the *Church Times*. *Practical Theology, 8*(2), 112–129.

Village, A., Baker, S., & Howat, S. (2012). Psychological type profiles of churchgoers in England. *Mental Health, Religion and Culture*, 15(10), 969–978.

Walker, D. S. (2012). O Come all ye thinking types: The wider appeal of the cathedral carol service. *Mental Health, Religion and Culture*, 15(10), 987–995.

Walker, D. S. (2015). Unsettling the Guardian: Quest religiosity and psychological type among Anglican churchgoers. *Mental Health, Religion and Culture*, 8, 655–663.

Westbury, J. I. (1975). *Religious beliefs and attitudes of pupils in an east London comprehensive school: factors influencing the pupils and implications for religious education*. Unpublished M.Ed. dissertation, University of Leicester.

West Riding (1966). *Suggestions for religious education: West Riding agreed syllabus*. Wakefield: County Council of the West Riding of Yorkshire.

White, J., Joseph, S., & Neil, A. (1995). Religiosity, psychoticism, and schizotypal traits. *Personality and Individual Differences*, 19, 847–851.

Whitehouse, E. (1972). Children's reactions to the Zacchaeus story. *Learning for Living*, 11(4), 19–24.

Wilcox, C., & Francis, L. J. (1997). Personality and religion among A level religious studies students. *International Journal of Children's Spirituality*, 1(2), 48–56.

Williams, E., & Francis, L. J. (2006). Personality and attitude toward Christianity among churchgoers: A replication. *Psychological Reports*, 99, 292–294.

Williams, E., Francis, L. J., & Robbins, M. (2006). Attitude toward Christianity and paranormal belief among 13- to 16-year-old students, *Psychological Reports*, 99, 266, 2006.

Williams, E., Robbins, M., & Francis, L. J. (2005). When introverts ceased to be more religious: A study among 12- to 16-year-old pupils. *Journal of Beliefs and Values*, 26, 77–79.

Williams, E., Robbins, M., & Francis, L. J. (2006). Personality and religion among adolescents in Wales. *The Psychologist in Wales*, 19, 21–22.

Wright, S. C., Aron, A., McLaughlin-Volpe, T., & Ropp, S. A. (1997). The extended contact effect: Knowledge of cross-group friendships and prejudice. *Journal of Personality and Social Psychology*, 73, 73–90.

Yablon, Y. B., Francis, L. J., & Robbins, M. (2014). The Katz-Francis Scale of Attitude toward Judaism: Internal consistency reliability and construct validity among female undergraduate students in Israel. *Pastoral Psychology*, 63, 73–78.

Youtika, A., Joseph, S., & Diduca, D. (1999). Personality and religiosity in a Greek Christian Orthodox sample. *Mental Health, Religion and Culture*, 2, 71–74.

Zhou, S., Page-Gould, E., Aron, A., Moyer, A., & Hewstone, M. (2019). The extended contact hypothesis: A meta-analysis on 20 years of research. *Personality and Social Psychology Review*, 23, 132–160.

Printed in the United States
By Bookmasters